Climate Conflict
How global warming threatens security and what to do about it

Jeffrey Mazo

Climate Conflict

How global warming threatens security and what to do about it

Jeffrey Mazo

IISS The International Institute for Strategic Studies

12354185

The International Institute for Strategic Studies

Arundel House | 13–15 Arundel Street | Temple Place | London | WC2R 3DX | UK

First published March 2010 by **Routledge**

4 Park Square, Milton Park, Abingdon, Oxon, OX14 4RN

for **The International Institute for Strategic Studies**

Arundel House, 13–15 Arundel Street, Temple Place, London, WC2R 3DX, UK
www.iiss.org

Simultaneously published in the USA and Canada by **Routledge**

270 Madison Ave., New York, NY 10016

Routledge is an imprint of Taylor & Francis, an Informa Business

© 2010 The International Institute for Strategic Studies

DIRECTOR-GENERAL AND CHIEF EXECUTIVE John Chipman
EDITOR Tim Huxley
MANAGER FOR EDITORIAL SERVICES Ayse Abdullah
ASSISTANT EDITOR Janis Lee
COVER/PRODUCTION/CARTOGRAPHY John Buck

The International Institute for Strategic Studies is an independent centre for research, information and debate on the problems of conflict, however caused, that have, or potentially have, an important military content. The Council and Staff of the Institute are international and its membership is drawn from almost 100 countries. The Institute is independent and it alone decides what activities to conduct. It owes no allegiance to any government, any group of governments or any political or other organisation. The IISS stresses rigorous research with a forward-looking policy orientation and places particular emphasis on bringing new perspectives to the strategic debate.

The Institute's publications are designed to meet the needs of a wider audience than its own membership and are available on subscription, by mail order and in good book-shops. Further details at www.iiss.org.

Printed and bound in Great Britain by Bell & Bain Ltd, Thornliebank, Glasgow

British Library Cataloguing in Publication Data
A catalogue record for this book is available from the British Library

Library of Congress Cataloging in Publication Data

ISBN 978-0-415-59118-8
ISSN 0567-932X

ADELPHI 409

Contents

ACKNOWLEDGEMENTS

I would like to thank Andrew Holland, Programme Manager and Research Associate for the IISS Transatlantic Dialogue on Climate Change and Security, as well as the participants in the Dialogue's workshops and seminars, for the stimulating and informative discussions; Cleo Paskal from Chatham House and Shiloh Fetzek from RUSI for our informal climate and security coffee klatches; Professor Michael Mann for his comments on an early draft of Chapter 1; my editorial and other colleagues at the IISS; and especially my wife Georgina, whose patience and editorial skills made this book possible. Any mistakes remain entirely my own.

INTRODUCTION

The scientific evidence leaves no doubt that the climate is changing in response to global warming.[1] In the past, climate change has affected the stability of societies, nations and civilisations, so the historically unprecedented change scientists are observing raises the spectre of increasing and accelerating social, geopolitical and economic disruption over the rest of this century and beyond. Crucially, climate change is not just one among myriad threats with which planners and policy-makers must deal; it can be in many cases a 'threat multiplier' that must be taken into account in policy debates on issues involving anything but the shortest timescales.[2]

Global warming has been on the radar for policy planners for some time. Empirical data on anthropogenic climate change were available as early as the 1930s, and various scientific advisory boards drew the potential problem to the attention of US presidents Lyndon Johnson, Richard Nixon and Jimmy Carter. The remoteness of the threat and uncertainty as to its likeliness and severity relegated it to the back burner,[3] but over the last few years it has acquired a sense of urgency. Some identify 2004 as the year 'climate change became respectable',[4] but interest was really catalysed by the publication in 2006 of former US Vice President Al Gore's best-selling book *An Inconvenient Truth* and release of the Academy Award-winning film of the same name. This was followed by a review of the economics of climate change commissioned by the UK Treasury (the Stern Review), and subsequently the Fourth Assessment Report of the United Nations Intergovernmental Panel on Climate Change (IPCC) in 2007.[5] Gore and the IPCC authors were jointly awarded the 2007 Nobel Peace Prize. That year also saw reports from at least four major security- or international-affairs think tanks on the question of climate change and security.[6] There were also warnings that climate change will lead to intra- and inter-state conflict over access to increasingly scarce resources from a growing list of academics, experts, and national and international leaders, among them British economist Nicholas Stern, UN Secretary-General Ban Ki-moon, French President Nicolas Sarkozy, UK Defence Secretary John Reid and Australian Prime Minister Kevin Rudd.[7] Similar warnings were sounded by UK Foreign Secretary Margaret Beckett before and during a UN Security Council debate on climate change and security, by the European Union, and by the Australian government's equivalent of the Stern Review.[8]

Yet significant questions and lacunae remain. These reports, assessments and statements, though in broad agreement as to the nature and scale of the security threat posed by climate change, often focus on worst-case rather than the most likely scenarios, look at a range of timescales, and can lack sufficient nuance or simply assume causal links. Many, in fact, are intended not so much to inform specific policy planning in response to identified threats, but to motivate policy choices that will avoid or ameliorate those threats. The outcome of the 2009 Copenhagen climate summit showed how difficult achieving such objectives, however necessary for long-term security, can be. But regardless of whether the longer-term threats can be avoided, there is a need to focus on policies aimed at adapting to the warming that will inevitably occur in the short to medium term.

A 2008 report from the German Advisory Council on Global Change (WBGU) identified a number of important priorities for future research on the climate–security nexus, including:

- bringing together findings from research into the underlying causes of conflict, violence and war, from research into environmental conflicts, from vulnerability research, from research on disaster management and on the reasons why governments and institutions fail to provide a basis for reconstructing the impacts of climate change on the stability of societies;
- empirical studies on the impact of climate change that differentiate between different types of society (such as democracies or autocracies) and different types of country (e.g. weak and fragile states) with differing levels of socioeconomic development; and
- closer communication between the social and natural sciences to inform research on the social impacts of climate change.[9]

This Adelphi book incorporates elements from all three of these priority areas. It is specifically intended to illustrate the social and security consequences of climate change that will manifest over the next two to three decades regardless of the policies adopted in the next few years to mitigate more severe impacts over the longer term. In effect, it assumes a best-case scenario in terms of international policy responses to climate change, though over the period in question there is little difference among the various projections of possible futures.

Given the failure of the Copenhagen conference in December 2009 to meet the deadline set two years earlier in Bali for a binding emissions regime to replace the 1997 Kyoto Protocol, this assumption may prove optimistic. The analysis relies on the IPCC Fourth Assessment Report and reviews of scientific research published after the IPCC cut-off date for the physical science and climate projections.

Since the end of the last Ice Age, climate and culture have marched hand in hand. From the beginnings of human civilisation climate change has been a key factor in the rise and fall of societies and states. It has been a driver of instability, conflict and collapse, but also of expansion and reorganisation. The ways cultures have met the challenge, for good or ill, provide object lessons for how we can face the security threats posed by the unprecedented warming we now face. How close the connection has been in specific cases is a matter of debate, but climate constantly emerges as one of myriad factors in a complex causal web underlying conflict from prehistory to the recent fighting in the Sudanese state of Darfur.

The expected consequences of climate change include rising sea levels and population displacement, increasing severity of typhoons and hurricanes, droughts, floods, disruption of water resources, extinctions and other ecological disruptions, wildfires, severe disease outbreaks, and declining crop yields and food stocks. Combining the historical precedents with current thinking on state stability, internal conflict and state failure suggests that adaptive capacity is the most important factor in avoiding climate-related instability. Specific global and regional climate projections for the next three decades, in light of other drivers of instability and state failure, help identify regions and countries which will see an increased risk from climate change. They are not necessarily the most fragile states, nor those which face the greatest physical effects of climate change.

The global security threat posed by fragile and failing states is well known. It is in the interest of the world's more affluent countries to take measures both to reduce the degree of global warming and climate change and to cushion the impact in those parts of the world where climate change will increase that threat. Neither course of action will be cheap, but inaction will be costlier. Efficient targeting of the right kind of assistance where it is most needed is one way of reducing the cost, and understanding how and why different societies respond to climate change is one way of making that possible.

CHAPTER ONE

Global Warming and Climate Change

This book is intended to help answer a simple question: what are the implications of climate change over the next few decades for global security and international relations? While the question may be simple, the answer is not. It touches on such complex and interrelated topics as the historical interaction between human society and climate, the dynamics of state stability and state failure, and the nexus between conflict and resource scarcity. Later chapters will consider examples of historical conflicts and societal failures induced, accelerated or intensified by resource scarcity and environmental factors; assess the relative risks of internal and inter-state conflict in different parts of the world; and discuss the probable consequences of climate-related instability and its implications for security policy of states and transnational organisations.

But these discussions are moot if we do not face significant changes in global and regional climate. How do we know change is occurring? Just how robust are the projections? And how severe will the changes be?

Ice Ages and hockey sticks: climate past and present

The evidence for global warming over the last 150 years is unambiguous, and the evidence that a substantial part of it was due to human activity is almost as certain.[1] The basic concept behind this explanation – the 'greenhouse effect' – is straightforward: the Earth's atmosphere retains heat because carbon dioxide (CO_2), water vapour and some other gases are relatively transparent to sunlight but less so to the frequencies at which energy is re-radiated from the warmed planet – analogous to the way a greenhouse retains heat. The mechanism is well understood; without it, the temperature of the Earth would be below freezing. The theory behind human-induced warming is that human activity – mainly the burning of fossil fuels, but also land-use patterns, farming and other practices – increases the concentration of these greenhouse gases in the atmosphere and thus reduces the amount of energy that is lost to space. In fact, it has been suggested that increasing human population and the spread of agriculture may go some way toward explaining why the last 5,000 years have seen a relatively mild and stable climate rather than a return to Ice Age conditions, as might have been expected on the basis of previous climate cycles.[2]

The IPCC's working group on the physical science of climate change concluded in 2007 that it was very likely that the rate of increase in the climate impact of the most important greenhouse gases over the last century was unique compared at least to the last 10,000 years. Variations in greenhouse-gas concentrations over this span, up to the Industrial Revolution, were smaller and mostly due to natural processes. It is unlikely that temporary warming episodes during this period, whether one-off or cyclical, were global in scope rather than limited to particular regions; nor can cyclical elements explain most of the recent warming.[3] The most visually compelling demonstration of the historical trends and the uniqueness of the present

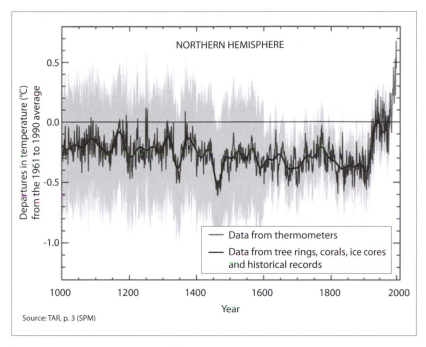

Figure 1. **The 'hockey stick' graph.**

The year by year (dark grey curve) and 50-year average (black curve) variations of the average surface temperature of the northern hemisphere for the past 1,000 years as reconstructed from tree rings, corals, ice cores and historical records and calibrated against thermometer data since 1850. The year by year curve since 1850 is based on the instrumental record. The 95% confidence range in the annual data is represented by the grey region.

is the so-called 'hockey-stick' graph of reconstructed mean northern hemisphere temperatures over the past millennium (Figure 1). This shows temperatures as relatively constant until the twentieth century (the shaft) with an abrupt, steep rise thereafter (the blade). Although it generated much controversy and criticism after it was published in 1999, precisely because it was so iconic, more recent reconstructions have confirmed it in all important respects and extended it to global coverage and backwards in time.[4] The graph is striking confirmation that the world is entering a historically unprecedented period of warming and climate instability.[5]

This is not to say that natural variations in climate are not important. Firstly, 'climate' by definition is simply weather averaged over at least several decades. The World Meteorological Organisation, for example, uses 30-year averages to identify climate trends.[6] This is because the difference in weather – temperature or precipitation – from one year to the next can be substantially greater than any underlying climate change. Annual variation thus risks swamping evidence of climate change when looked at over too short a period. Random events such as volcanic eruptions can also have significant short-term cooling effects that can mask long-term trends.

Besides these random or chaotic fluctuations, there are also weather cycles on various time scales which themselves vary in length and severity, so climate must be considered over a period long enough to subsume several such cycles. The most important is the two- to seven-year cycle of fluctuation in the El Niño–Southern Oscillation (ENSO) system, a coupling of global-scale tropical and sub-tropical atmospheric pressure patterns with tropical Pacific surface temperatures. A period of unusually high sea-surface temperatures in the tropical Pacific is called 'El Niño' and its colder mirror image is 'La Niña'. These can have widespread effects on temperature and precip- itation patterns, including monsoons, and lead to droughts and floods. What some people argue has been a levelling-off of global warming since 1998 is merely an artefact of a strong El Niño effect in that year, a perfect example of the need to consider climate over periods of several decades. There is no consensus on whether the variations on the scale of centuries or millennia apparent in the original hockey-stick graph and its analogues are cyclical or random.

These sorts of uncertainties have been cited by some policy advocates and policymakers and in the media as reasons to dismiss the potential threat of climate change or to delay unpopular or expensive policy responses.[7] But the conclusions of the IPCC – that there is no doubt that there has been global warming over the last 100 years, that it accelerated in the second half of the twentieth century and that most of it is very likely due to increased concentrations of man-made greenhouse gases – reflects the consensus of the international scientific community. A study of 928 scientific papers published between 1993 and 2003, designed to test the idea that the IPCC assessment reports (among others) might downplay legitimate dissenting views, concluded that any impression of confusion, disagreement or discord among climate scientists was incorrect.[8] The very small number of vocal contrarian scientists, not all of them climatologists, does not belie 'the basic reality [that] anthropogenic global climate change is no longer a subject of scientific debate'.[9]

A more recent survey found that 82% of Earth scientists and 97.4% of climatologists agreed human activity was a significant contributing factor in changing global temperatures. The authors concluded 'the debate on the authenticity of global warming and the role played by human activity is largely nonexistent among those who understand the nuances and scientific basis of long-term climate processes'.[10] Whether that consensus is correct is a separate question, which cannot be addressed by criticism or falsification of individual studies or data sets. Climate science, and hence the current consensus on anthropogenic global warming, is firmly grounded in a consilience of method, evidence and theory.[11]

The IPCC is, if anything, prone to underestimate the likely human contribution to global warming and the severity of its impacts. The conservative and consensual assessment process guards against over-reliance on individual studies or personalities on either side of the debate.[12] The robust nature of the methods and conclusions is reflected in the reduction in uncertainty between the IPCC's Third Assessment Report in 2001 and the Fourth in 2007. For example, the precision and margin

of error in the estimates of the rise in global mean temperature in the twentieth century both improved, and a better and
lower estimate of the contribution of changes in solar radiation
to temperature change in the post-industrial period was also
obtained.[13] More generally, advances in detecting and attrib-
uting recent climate change, understanding climate processes,
and modelling climate have all led to more robust results not
just since 2001 but progressively since the first assessment
report in 1990.[14]

The controversy over the hockey-stick graph exemplifies
this process. Published in 1999, it was used to illustrate the
Third Assessment Report and came to be an iconic symbol of
the anthropogenic global-warming hypothesis. It thus became
a lightning rod for climate-change sceptics, who argued it was
based on bad data, was unreliable due to uncertainties associated with the wide range of proxy data (tree rings, pollen
deposition, air bubbles in ice, etc.), and was a statistical artefact.[15] It was the focus of two reports commissioned by members
of the US Congress in response to the controversy. One, a peer-
reviewed report from the National Research Council, generally
affirmed its methods and conclusions; the other was sharply
critical.[16] Yet each of the criticisms levelled at the hockey stick
has been independently rebutted and the original authors of
the graph have refined and extended their work.[17] After all this
give-and-take it is now widely agreed that the hockey stick is
consistent with the overall scientific consensus on past climate
trends; it is one of 12 reconstructions compiled in the IPCC
Fourth Assessment Report.[18]

The progressive refinement of the scientific consensus which
can be seen over the course of the four assessments points to
another inherently conservative aspect of the IPCC process.
The complexity of the process, with hundreds of scientists
involved in assessing thousands of published studies, meant

the cut-off date for a s[...]
a report approved in F[...]
and published in Nov[...]
account research pu[...]
Although the assess[...]
comprehensive an[...]
edge about climat[...]
further work had
indicates that, if
projections und[...]
anthropogenic climate [...]

The terms 'global wa[...]
used interchangeabl[...]
can be politically [...]
sides of a polic[...]
opposite reas[...]
tant distin[...]
observe[...]
plane[...]
the[...]

Projections and policy: climate future

In February 2007 the IPCC's physical sciences working group reported that global warming, which had been averaging 0.13°C per decade over the previous 50 years, would continue over the next two decades at a rate of around 0.2°C per decade, regardless of which set of assumptions were taken for trends in the greenhouse-gas emissions responsible for the rise.[20] Even if the increase in concentrations of greenhouse gases in the atmosphere could be stopped entirely, warming would still continue at about half that rate. The best estimates of temperature change by the end of the century ranged from 1.8–4.0°C depending on the scenario, with likely ranges running from 1.1–2.9°C to 2.4–6.4°C. (These ranges exemplify the uncertainties in climate projection.) Even with concentrations held constant, the world faces a rise of 0.6°C (0.3–0.9°C) over this period. To put these figures in context, the globe warmed by 0.74°C (0.56–0.92°C) between 1906 and 2005, mostly during the last 50 years. Further increases of 1–2°C above 1990–2000 levels would have a net negative effect on most people.[21] Climate change will not be uniform, but will vary from region to region.[22]

rming' and 'climate change' are often
. The choice of one term over the other
motivated, although advocates on opposite
issue will often use the same vocabulary for
ons. But in fact the terms do allow some impor-
tions. 'Global warming' is simple shorthand for the
increase in the average annual temperature of the
over the last two centuries or so, and its projection into
future. This increase has been around 0.76°C (0.57–0.95°C)
since 1850–1899 – the earliest period for which direct measure-
ments are available. This may seem ludicrously small compared
to the differences in temperature we experience every day,
between day and night, across seasons or between different
regions even within a single country. This is because average
values obscure more complex and subtle changes in precisely
such measures. 'Climate change' covers these aspects, as well as
those not related to temperature, such as precipitation, climate
stability and frequency of extreme events.

The use of the term 'global warming', moreover, obscures
one of the most important features of climate change. Climate
change has been and will continue to be far from uniform
around the world: it shows great variation from region to
region. The anticipated climate change in any particular part
of the globe is driven not just by average warming but by
changes in global ocean and atmospheric circulation patterns
that directly impact climate by, for example, strengthening or
weakening monsoons. Cyclical patterns like ENSO can also be
strengthened or weakened, and more persistent geographic
shifts in climate zones can occur, as they have in the past. The
most basic difference is between land and water: continents
will warm more than seas, and continental interiors will warm
more than areas close to the ocean. The amount of warming,
too, tends to vary by latitude, with higher latitudes projected

to warm more, and according to factors such as the presence of large mountain ranges, which also affect precipitation.[23]

Precipitation patterns in particular will vary significantly, in terms of both total amount and the chronological distribution and intensity of precipitation events. Although, overall, precipitation is expected to increase with global warming, within this global average some regions could see declines. For example, for projections to the end of the century under one scenario, the best estimate for global temperature increase is 2.8°C.[24] However, the median annual temperature increase ranges from 1.8–4.9°C depending on region. The projected increase is 2.5°C or less for Southeast Asia, southern South America, and the small island states of the Caribbean, tropical northeast Atlantic, Indian Ocean and Pacific, and more than 4°C for the Arctic and adjoining regions such as northern Asia, Alaska, eastern Canada, Greenland and Iceland. Within particular regions, the projected increase can vary by as little as 0.2°C or as much as 4.8°C between seasons.[25]

Projections of regional-climate change impacts are less robust than those for the world as a whole, because of the resolution of models, scaling effects and local geography.[26] Improving such projections is among the most important and active areas of climate research, but at present the state of the art is comparable to the state of global-warming science as it stood some 10–20 years ago. Even with the current models and methods, moreover, making such projections is not inexpensive in manpower and other resources, and for many parts of the world projections even at the level of detail permitted by current understanding are not available. The best regional studies so far are, understandably, for the wealthier industrialised countries which can afford to conduct the research.[27] These countries are, of course, in a better position to adapt to climate change than most, especially in the short to medium term, and their ability to gather and analyse data and make projections is one aspect of this adaptive capacity. Some work has also been done on impacts in the poorest regions or those indicated by broader global studies as being at the greatest risk, although it is not necessarily up to date. Countries that fall in between the extremes have been relatively neglected.

Between the short-term (one- to two-week) scale of reasonably accurate weather forecasts and the long-term (multi-decadal to century) climate projections such as those produced by the IPCC lies a gap of particular interest to policymakers and planners. The timescale for long-term national-security and defence planning and force-structure development, for example, tends to be 10–30 years. But chaotic, random and cyclical factors make it extremely difficult to project or identify climate trends on scales shorter than 30 years. Only in the last few years have scientists begun to investigate the feasibility of producing useful medium-term forecasts. This work is in its early stages – like regional projections, it is perhaps where long-term climate projections were 20 years ago – but is expected to be a key component of the next IPCC assessment report. The preliminary results are interesting. The ocean tends to act as a 'short-term memory' for the climate system, with unusually warm or cool spots persisting for years, and the currents that move heat around the world are also subject to variation on this scale.[28] One group predicts that over the next decade variations in oceanic circulation in the North Atlantic could produce sufficient cooling in Europe, North America and the tropical Pacific to offset – temporarily – the warming trend from greenhouse emissions.[29] Another achieved similar results, but suggests a temporary slowing rather than a reversal of warming over the next decade.[30] Although it will never be possible to overcome all the inherent uncertainty in medium-term forecasts, nor to anticipate random factors such as volcanic eruptions that might alter the forecasts, their accuracy is likely to improve significantly over the next five to ten years.[31]

Projecting climate change over longer periods depends more strongly on the underlying assumptions about social and political variables, and there is greater variability across a range of models and methods compared to short-term projections.[32] The 'sweet spot', where the degree of uncertainty relative to the level of projected warming is minimised, is around 2040 for global projections and 2060 for at least one regional projection.[33] But since the uncertainty persists in spite of the general agreement of all climate-projection scenarios for the next two decades, policymakers and planners will in the meantime have to focus on promoting or maintaining the flexibility to cope with a range of possible climate developments.

The IPCC projections in the Fourth Assessment Report are based on illustrative scenarios taken from six scenario groups based on four 'narrative storylines' representing different demographic, social, economic and environmental developments outlined in the *IPCC Special Report on Emissions Scenarios* (SRES).[34] One of these, the A1FI scenario group, represents a fossil-fuel-intensive, market-oriented and rapidly growing world economy, with global population peaking in 2050 and subsequently declining. It is commonly known as 'business-as-usual' (BAU). The SRES scenarios have been widely adopted by scientists, as they make comparison between different models and studies easier; other scenario approaches currently in use apply similar assumptions.[35] The scenarios are not designed to be taken as predictions, but to provide a range of possibilities, and there are no built-in assumptions that any of the scenarios is more likely than another. Nor are the best-case and worst-case scenarios at the extreme ends of what might actually happen; they are best or worst only in the context of the other scenarios. It is self-evident, too, that the various scenarios are not equally likely, even if it is not possible to assign them relative probabilities. Moreover, policymakers can affect the relative likelihood of the different futures through their decisions. To say the scenarios do not take into account mitigation efforts and other than spontaneous adaptation efforts is somewhat disingenuous, since different mitigation and adaptation policies are what could make one scenario more likely than another. Adaptation takes place across a range of social, time- and geographic scales, with complex interactions between them, which means the distinction between spontaneous and policy-driven adaptation is not of great help.

The recent emissions trend has tracked the worst-case SRES scenario. If it continues to follow this path, the human and geopolitical consequences later in the century will be extreme. Strong mitigating action needs to be taken in the next few years to avert this outcome. But even the strongest efforts cannot avoid some warming still in the pipeline from past emissions, and the warming projections across the range of SRES scenarios do not actually differ greatly over the next 20–30 years, globally or regionally. The mean global temperature for 2011–2030 is projected to be 0.64–0.69°C above the mean for 1980–1999, consistent with the trend over the last few decades.[36] For land areas the temperature increase for 2020–2040 will be roughly 1°C over 1980–1999 in most regions.[37] By 2030 the amount by which the average temperature over every continent except Antarctica is expected to rise each decade is very likely to be at least twice as large as the range within which average temperatures might be expected to vary naturally.[38]

Mitigation, in this context, means efforts, such as the Kyoto Protocol, intended to limit or reduce the level of greenhouse-gas emissions and their atmospheric concentrations, and hence the overall level and rate of warming (Article 2 of the UN's Framework Convention on Climate Change (UNFCCC) calls

Emphasis on growth	

A1 – Global growth and convergence
• Rapid economic growth
• Population peaks at mid-century
• Capacity building
• Narrowing GDP gap
• Rapid introduction of new, efficient technologies
  • **A1FI (BAU):** Fossil-fuel intensive
  • **A1T:** Non-fossil energy sources
  • **A1B:** Balance across all sources
	A2 – A heterogenous world
	• Self-reliance and preservation of local identities
	• Continuously increasing global population
	• Economic development is primarily regionally oriented
	• Per capita economic growth and technological change are more fragmented and slower than in other storylines.

B1 – Global solutions and sustainability • Population peaks at mid-century • Rapid change towards service and information economy • Reductions in material intensity • Clean and resource-efficient technologies • Improved equity (Best-case emissions scenario)	**B2 – Local solutions and sustainability** • Continuously increasing global population (lower than A2) • Intermediate levels of economic development • Less rapid and more diverse technological development • Focus on environmental protection and social equality
Emphasis on sustainability	

Global emphasis (left) — Regional emphasis (right)

Source: 4AR WG1, p. 18 (SPM).

Figure 2. **The SRES emissions scenarios and their socio-economic assumptions.**

for stabilisation of concentrations at a level and rate that would 'prevent dangerous anthropogenic interference with the climate system'[39]). By contrast, adaptation covers changes in behaviour – individual, collective or technological – to minimise the negative impacts of what climate change does occur despite mitigation efforts. Spontaneous adaptation is adaptation by individuals that takes place without specific policy initiatives. For example, if farmers find they lack sufficient irrigation water for a particular crop, or seasonal temperatures affect the growth of a particular crop, they will not, if they have the choice, simply sit and watch their yields decline – they will plant a different crop, or change their irrigation method, etc.

The line between spontaneous and policy-directed adaptation can be fuzzy; on the most basic level adaptation programmes can simply comprise information campaigns about what crops are most appropriate in the changed circumstances. But of course adaptation can extend to large-scale infrastructure-renewal projects, such as strengthening sea defences and public health systems. One of the key variables in assessing the overall impact of climate change is the capacity of individual nations and societies to adapt, which depends both on their innate capacity and the magnitude and rate of climate change.[40]

The range of possible atmospheric concentrations and rates of emission of greenhouse gases in the various scenarios is not the only source of uncertainty in making long-term climate projections. The changes in radiative forcing (see endnote 3) produced by changes in greenhouse-gas concentrations are also subject to uncertainties. The computer models used to project future climate are one source. These models, complex computer programs involving large numbers of variables, are considered reliable because of the underlying theory, their accuracy with respect to current climate and their ability to reproduce historical climate changes. However, they are generally less reliable on regional or local scales than they are for global climate, and scientists are forced by lack of knowledge, data or computing power to use approximations for many physical processes in making projections at all scales. As a result, although different models consistently agree on significant climate change in response to greenhouse gases, they produce different estimates for regional details as well as how much warming there will be and how fast it will occur.[41]

This latter aspect, the rate of change, is a critical factor in terms of adapting to climate change. Although some states and societies will be better able to adapt to change than others, regardless of how resilient a given society is there will always be some point at which its efforts would be overwhelmed by the pace of change.

Changes in climate – long-term wind and rainfall patterns, daily and seasonal temperature variations, and so on – will produce physical effects such as droughts, floods and increasing severity of typhoons and hurricanes, and ecological effects such as changes in the geographical range of species (including disease-causing organisms, domesticated crops and crop pests). These physical changes in turn may lead to effects such as disruption of water resources, declining crop yields and food stocks, wildfires, severe disease outbreaks, and an increase in numbers of refugees and internally displaced persons.[42]

Beyond such impacts, which are expected to increase in severity in line with increasing temperatures globally or regionally, there is potential for sudden, non-linear impacts, where the Earth–climate system reaches a tipping point and rapidly shifts into a new state. Both the scale and the suddenness of such changes could be devastating. For example, at the end of the last Ice Age, melting of the North American ice sheet produced what geologists call Lake Agassiz, a vast freshwater lake that was, at its largest, around seven times the size of the modern Great Lakes put together. As the lake formed gradually from the melting ice cap, it was prevented from draining by ice dams, which themselves periodically collapsed as temperatures continued to rise, sending pulses of fresh water into the North Atlantic. Three of the largest pulses, around 12,900, 11,300 and 8,200 years ago, coincided with a sudden reversion to colder, glacial conditions in the northern hemisphere that lasted for centuries. Although the climate began to stabilise from around 10,000 years ago, the final collapse of the Lake Agassiz ice dam around 8,200 years ago was by far the largest, and the climate shifts it induced had a major impact on human cultures and civilisations around the world. As a result,

A human epoch?

Scientists divide Earth history into a descending hierarchy of time units: eons, eras, periods, epochs and ages. We are currently in the Quarternary period of the Cenozoic era. The epoch of relatively stable climate from around 11,700 years ago to the present is called the Holocene. There have been 12 eras lasting hundreds of millions of years, while the Pleistocene, the epoch preceding the Holocene, lasted around 2.5 million years. The divisions are derived from observed discontinuities in the geological and fossil record, many if not all of which correspond to major changes in global climate.

Some scientists argue that the human impact on global climate since the beginning of the Industrial Revolution is so significant as to merit a new geological epoch, the Anthropocene, and even a new geological era. One scholar has even suggested that the start of the Anthropocene should be pushed back to the beginning of agriculture some 8,000 years ago – a suggestion which essentially obviates the concept of separate Holocene and Anthropocene epochs.

Sources: International Commission on Stratigraphy, *International Strategic Chart 2008*, available at http://www.stratigraphy.org/; P.J. Crutzen and E.F. Stoermer, 'The "Anthropocene"', *Global Change Newsletter*, no. 41, May 2000, pp. 17–18; William F. Ruddiman, 'The Anthropogenic Greenhouse Era Began Thousands of Years Ago', *Climatic Change*, vol. 61, no. 3, December 2003, pp. 261–93.

during the transition from Ice Age conditions to the Holocene – the geological term for the epoch of relatively stable climate from around 11,700 years ago to the present – the climate in the northern hemisphere acted like a 'flickering switch', with average temperatures and precipitation patterns fluctuating wildly over periods of only a few years.[43] If the modern climate were to become similarly chaotic, agriculture would be limited to refugia in the 'most blessed parts of the world'.[44]

Besides the extreme variability of weather, potential non-linear impacts include abrupt sea-level rise and regional cooling – for the same reasons such cooling occurred periodically at the end of the last Ice Age, through shut-down of warm ocean currents such as the Gulf Stream due to infusion of cold, fresh meltwater from the ice caps[45] – as well as massive disruption of ecosystems, for example die-back of the Amazon rain forest; disruption of the monsoon in South Asia and West Africa; disruption of the ENSO; permanent melting of Arctic sea-ice and permafrost; and release of marine methane hydrates, which would significantly multiply and accelerate global warming.[46] These potential impacts are 'abrupt' in the sense that they occur much faster than the underlying temperature changes that induce them, but they nevertheless would be expected to take anywhere from a decade to a century or more to reach full effect. None of these non-linear impacts is considered likely in this century. Nonetheless, even if the level of confidence of such projections is low, the consequences are high.[47]

The climate threat

Climate change has traditionally been viewed in the international diplomatic arena as an environmental issue. The IPCC itself, established in 1988, was a child of the UN's World Meteorological Organisation (WMO) and United Nations Environment Programme (UNEP). Its first assessment report in 1990 was instrumental in the establishment of the UNFCCC, which was opened for signature at the Rio Earth Summit in June 1992. Although many heads of state attended the summit, much of its work and that of its follow-up meetings was under the remit of national environment ministers. When the UN Security Council debated climate change and security in April 2007 under the aegis of the United Kingdom's presidency, many nations (including China, Russia and Pakistan, the latter representing a large group of developing countries) objected that climate change was an environmental and developmental issue, not a security issue, and that the council was not the appropriate place to debate it – in fact, that such a debate was an encroachment on the prerogatives of other UN organs.

Climate only began to be widely securitised in the policy arena around 2005–2006. There were, to be sure, academic debates and isolated voices before then; but of the 73 items on climate change and national security in an annotated list compiled by a United States Air Force Air University research centre bibliographer in

April 2008, 80% were published in 2005 or later, and over 65% in 2007–2008 alone.[48] This trend may have been catalysed by the widespread popularisation of the climate issue through the release in 2006 of former Vice President Al Gore's documentary 'An Inconvenient Truth' and his book of the same title, and the release of the IPCC's Fourth Assessment Report in 2007. In recognition of the importance of these two major publications, one aimed at the general public and the other at policymakers, Gore and the IPCC shared the 2007 Nobel Peace Prize.

Several influential security and foreign-policy think tanks released reports on climate change and security in 2007. In April, the day before the UN Security Council debate, the CNA Corporation published, with the oversight of a panel of 11 retired generals and admirals and under the direction of a former undersecretary of defense for environmental security, a widely publicised study that concluded that projected climate change over the next 30–40 years posed a serious threat to US national security. It would, said the report, act as a 'threat multiplier' for instability in volatile regions and add to tensions in more stable regions.[49] In September the International Institute for Strategic Studies in London highlighted the issue in its annual *Strategic Survey*,[50] and in November the Center for Strategic and International Studies (CSIS) and the Center for a New American Security (CNAS) published a joint report looking at three climate-change scenarios: expected, severe and catastrophic. The CSIS/CNAS study concluded that even the expected climate change scenario, 'the least we ought to prepare for', would see 'heightened internal and cross-border tensions caused by large-scale migrations; [and] conflict sparked by resource scarcity, particularly in the weak and failing states of Africa'.[51] Also in November, The Council on Foreign Relations published a Special Report on climate change and national security, citing both the CNA and CSIS/CNAS studies.[52]

While the problems highlighted in these reports are real and significant, the impetus for the securitisation of climate change in public discourse, especially through longer-term and more severe scenarios, may have been in part due to a desire on the part of policy advocates to highlight the self-interest of policymakers and their constituents. If so, they were successful. In a speech at Chatham House in London as early as February 2006, then UK Defence Secretary John Reid warned the armed forces would have to be prepared – and were planning – to cope with conflicts in the developing world over scarce resources in the face of climate change over the next 20–30 years.[53] In May 2007 the US Congress commissioned a classified National Intelligence Estimate (NIE) on the security implications of climate change (delivered in June 2008), and directed that the 2010 Quadrennial Defense Review address climate security. In March 2007, in his first major address after taking office, UN Secretary-General Ban Ki-moon said there was an urgent need to reframe the debate on climate change from an environmental to a development and security issue, and that it would be one of his top priorities as secretary-general.[54] On the eve of the Security Council debate six weeks later, then UK Foreign Secretary Margaret Beckett gave the Annual Winston Churchill Memorial Lecture in New York. Alluding to the US NIE about to be approved by Congress, and the CNA report published that morning, she compared the security implications of climate change to a 'gathering storm' – the title of Churchill's volume on the build-up to world war in the 1930s.[55] A year later, EU foreign-policy chief Javier Solana and European Commissioner for External Relations Benita Ferrero-Waldner issued a report on 'Climate Change and International Security' in advance of an EU summit, concluding that climate change was 'a threat multiplier which ... threatens to overburden states and regions which are already fragile and conflict prone'.[56] A month after the EU summit, at a Major Economies Meeting in April, French President Nicolas Sarkozy said climate change was already driving instability, conflict and war.[57] He cited the fighting in the Sudanese state of Darfur. As a final example, in February 2009 Nicholas Stern, author of the 2006 UK review on the economics of climate change, warned at a meeting of environment ministers, diplomats and climate experts in Cape Town that without decisive action to deal with climate change the world could face extended war: 'somehow we have to explain to people just how worrying that is'.[58] Thus, over a period of around three years, the analytical literature had reached critical mass and the conventional wisdom in policy circles had shifted from global warming as a scientific question and environmental issue to climate change as a real and present security threat.

Beneath these analytical syntheses and political statements is another, more fundamental layer of research focussing on correlations and causal links between environmental conditions and change and social and political developments that impact security – from economic impacts that affect domestic politics to inter-ethnic or other intra-state violence and inter-state conflicts. Moving from empirical research to synthesis to political discourse involves increasing abstraction at each stage, and there is a danger that nuance will be lost. For example, Ban Ki-moon, in his *Washington Post* op-ed in June 2007 arguing that 'amid the diverse social and political causes, the Darfur conflict began as an ecological crisis, arising at least in part from climate change',[59] cited two sources: Columbia University economist Jeffrey Sachs (one of his advisers) and an article by journalist Stephan Faris in *The Atlantic* a few months earlier.[60] Yet Faris, in turn, relied heavily on the research and experiences of anthropologist Alex de Waal in Darfur in the 1980s. In a response to Ban Ki-moon, de Waal broke down the putative climate–conflict link into a causal chain and examined each link in detail. He concluded:

> Ban Ki-moon's linking of climate change and the Darfur crisis is simplistic. Climate change causes livelihood change, which in turn causes disputes. Social institutions can handle these conflicts and settle them in a non-violent manner – it is mismanagement and militarization that cause war and massacre.[61]

An analysis of rainfall patterns and conflict in the Sahel by two University of California researchers provides some empirical support for this conclusion.[62]

The particular example of Darfur will be revisited and analysed in greater detail later; the important point here is that while there is a danger of assuming a simplistic, deterministic connection between environmental problems, especially those induced or exacerbated by climate change, and conflict and security threats, there is conversely a danger that the contribution of climate change to current or potential conflicts might be downgraded or ignored out of a mistaken belief that environmental causes somehow absolve individuals and governments from responsibility for their actions. De Waal was responding less to Ban Ki-moon's article, which did in fact discuss 'diverse social and political causes', than to a straw man of his own making. Both de Waal and Ban Ki-moon recognise that the conflict had multiple and interacting causes, both ultimate and proximate; they really differ only in the emphasis they place on particular causes in order to advance particular policy responses. Although the higher level of abstraction involved in viewing the climate–security nexus holistically can sometimes appear to over-simplify the links, as a move from the tactical to the strategic it can reveal connections and suggest new policy needs and approaches.

Environment and culture

Climate security – the security considerations of both static and changing climates – is an aspect of environmental security. This relationship manifests in two ways. The primary physical and ecological impacts of climate change are environmental impacts, but climate change is also an exacerbating factor or multiplier of pre-existing environmental problems, themselves – like the accelerating greenhouse-gas emissions that cause anthropogenic global warming – due ultimately to the demands of economic growth and population pressure. Environmental constraints have had broad effects on the development of human societies, cultures and civilisations.

In China, for example, early agriculture began to expand beyond the semi-arid regions of loess soil (with millet as a staple crop) to the flood plain of the Yellow River around 600 BCE. This involved new agricultural and flood-control techniques and technologies and large-scale development of rice paddies. The expanded food resources sustained 400 years of warfare – the 'warring states period' – until the whole of China was conquered by the Ch'in state in 221 BCE and the Han dynasty consolidated control in 202 BCE. Although nominally under the control of the central imperial authorities, similar agricultural development did not occur in the Yangtze River Valley to the south for another five or six centuries. In his seminal work on the history of disease William McNeill argued that the sharp climatic difference between the colder, drier Yellow River Valley in the north and the warmer, moister Yangtze in central China created a steep disease gradient that formed a real barrier to expansion of Chinese civilisation.[63] China, moreover, developed a mostly stable centralised government while the Ganges Valley in India, a region even warmer and wetter than central China, was never consolidated politically, in part because of the heavier disease burden that stemmed from its own climatic conditions.[64]

Similarly, the climate-dependent ecology of malaria and the tsetse fly had a profound impact on human development in sub-Saharan Africa.[65] Taking an even broader view, anthropologist Jared Diamond argued in his masterful *Guns, Germs and Steel* that the ultimate reason the West came to dominate Africa, Asia and the Americas, and not the other way around, was environmental: Europe and Western Asia had a favourable continental geography and better plant and animal species available for domestication.[66]

Environmental constraints were recognised in antiquity,[67] but the first modern scholar to develop a coherent theory of environmental factors as a driver of history was Ellsworth Huntington, who published *The Pulse of Asia* in 1907 and elaborated his theories in *Climate and Civilisation* in 1915.[68] He argued that the main northern hemisphere storm track periodically shifted north or south, changing the distribution of rainfall. This produced cyclical periods of desiccation in the Mediterranean and the Central Asian steppe, creating the 'pulse of Asia' in which migrating tribes periodically erupted from their steppe homeland in search of new resources – at a time Mediterranean civilisations were themselves weakened by reduced rainfall. An early pulse led to expansion of the Indo-European speakers; a later pulse to the migrations of Germanic, Celtic, Slavic and Turkic tribes (the latter including the Huns) that overwhelmed the Roman Empire from the third century CE onwards.[69] It is notable that Huntington was writing around the same time, and may well have been influenced by, H.J. Mackinder, whose seminal geopolitical theories involved a similar abstraction at global and continental scales.[70] While the theories of both scholars have been discarded in their details, they still inform more nuanced modern analyses of international relations on the global scale.

Environmental theories of history began to revive in the 1970s – McNeill's analysis of the effect of disease on history is a prime example – but they were often derided as 'environmental determinism' by critics. For the most part, though, they were not strictly deterministic but rather, as in the debate over the causes of the Darfur crisis, simply a re-orientation of emphasis towards an important factor that had been given insufficient weight or even neglected entirely.

Environment and conflict

Over the last 20 years, three broad research approaches to the nexus between environment and conflict have emerged: case-based methodologies used by the Toronto group around the Toronto Project on Environmental Change and Acute Conflict under Thomas Homer-Dixon and the Zurich group around the Environment and Conflicts Project at the Swiss Federal Institute of Technology, and the quantitative approach of the Oslo group around the International Peace Research Institute Oslo (PRIO) under Otto Gleditsch.[71] The various approaches have produced broad agreement in a number of areas:

- Environmental factors are only one, and rarely the decisive, contribution to a complex interaction of other political, social and economic factors underlying conflict. The adaptive and problem-solving capacity of a state or society is perhaps the most critical factor affecting whether environmental crises will lead to conflict.
- There is no evidence to date that environmental problems have been a *direct* cause of inter-state warfare. Conflicts involving environmental factors occur predominantly within states, and where they do transcend state borders they tend to be sub-national rather than classic inter-state conflicts.[72]

The main specific security threats from climate change – beyond general systemic weakening – as identified by analysts and policymakers fall into the three broad categories: resource wars, state instability, and boundary disputes due to rising sea levels and melting of the arctic ice. The first of these does not appear, from the primary literature, to be a major factor at levels of climate change to be expected in the next 10–30 years, and would probably manifest only in the event of severe non-linear impacts or unmitigated emissions growth, perhaps over the course of at least a century. The third factor is unprecedented and may well be an issue, but depends on rate and degree of sea-level rise (and is thus also a longer-term threat). Being primarily a political rather than an economic issue, it is more amenable than most climate threats to a political solution. The more immediate threat of rising sea levels is as an exacerbating factor for extreme weather events, agricultural impacts and population displacement – thus acting as another of the stress multipliers that could affect state stability.

The two areas where there is a broad consensus among analysts – the multi-causal nature of violent conflict and relative sensitivity of inter- and intra-state conflict to environmental factors – are a starting point. To disaggregate multiple, complex causation (where important factors may be neither necessary nor sufficient causal factors) and thereby clarify the circumstances under which climate change may contribute to instability, conflict and state failure, the appropriate approach is case based and comparative.[73]

Environment and security

Security is more than just the avoidance of violent conflict. Since the end of the Cold War the broad concept of security in international discourse has expanded to cover 'human security' – personal, economic, and so on – and the development of environmental security as a field has been part of this. But this goes to the very heart of the question of what constitutes 'dangerous anthropogenic influence' in the climate system, and the question of securitising – in the classic sense – the climate issue.

Much recent criticism of environmental conflict research is based on objections involving the attribution of blame (absolving individuals and repressive regimes of responsibility for, to give one example, the Darfur conflict) and the danger of diverting resources to the military from urgent, existing development problems such as poverty, lack of education, HIV/AIDS, human rights, and so on.[74] Similar objections have been raised that policies to enable adaptation to climate change draw attention and resources from necessary mitigation efforts. But the argument is not that 'ecology is destiny' – that there is a deterministic relationship between environmental stresses and violence – but rather that environment (and climate in particular) is one of manifold and non-essential causal factors, and that disaggregating its contribution is valuable as a step towards developing policies that can enhance human security.

If 'dangerous' means 'security-threatening', it can apply to human security, security of the Westphalian nation-state, security and continuity of the international state system, or continuity of enlightenment liberalism or other ideological or economic systems. A culture or civilisation can survive despite horrific losses in human terms (for example, the Soviet Union became one of the twentieth century's two superpowers despite losing 6–7 million people in the famines of the 1930s and around 30m in the Second World War, or up to 15% of its population).[75] On the other hand, a 'culture' – defined by physical artefacts and expressive culture, and reflecting underlying ideology – can disappear almost over night without major human losses (the 'collapse' of the Soviet Union in 1989–1990 was political, cultural and ideological, but relatively benign in human terms[76]). While by no means intending to downplay the importance of the other aspects, the present work focuses on security from the perspective of the nation-state and the international system.

CHAPTER TWO

Climate and History

The fates of societies and civilisations have always been intimately connected to climate. The interaction of climate and geography has influenced the broad trajectory of human history in several ways and on scales from local to continental. Climate affects distribution of plant and animal species available for domestication; the productivity of agriculture, in terms of growing rates and seasons, soil formation, and of the presence or absence of diseases and pests; and the ecology of human disease.[1]

Indeed, climate fluctuations are fundamental to the intellectual framework used to characterise human prehistory. The divisions in the geological timescale are defined by discontinuities in the fossil record – that is, by major changes in the environment and ecosystem – which often reflect major climatic shifts. For example, the current epoch, the Holocene, covering the last 10,000 years, was originally defined in the nineteenth century by reference to the change in vegetation at the end of the most recent Ice Age, as revealed in Scandinavian peat bogs. Between 14,000 and 9,500 BCE, as the climate began to warm, most of the largest animals (or megafauna) – mammoths, rhinoceroses, giant deer, etc. – of North America, Europe and northern Eurasia became extinct. There is a general consensus that climate change was largely responsible for these extinctions, but as these species had survived previous interglacials many scientists believe a new factor – over-hunting by humans – was also an important cause.[2]

At the same time forests began to spread and greater plant food resources became available. People began first to exploit these wild resources, then to plant and cultivate their own. Although human cultural development occurred at different times between and within regions, the start of the Holocene broadly corresponds with the transition to the culturally defined Neolithic, generally characterised by permanent human settlements, domestication of plants and animals, and the use of pottery. In many areas, including Northern Europe, the Neolithic was preceded by a cultural phase called the Mesolithic, characterised by semi-permanent settlement, increased exploitation of estuarine and maritime food resources, and a flourishing of new bone, stone and wood technologies. Because much of the pioneering archaeological work of the nineteenth century was done in Northern Europe, the material-cultural transitions of that region – Paleolithic–Mesolithic–Neolithic–Bronze Age–Iron Age – became the general framework under which global prehistory was categorised. The length, or even existence, of the Mesolithic phase in a particular region or sub-region appears to depend on the local climate transitions.[3]

The earliest evidence for agriculture comes from the Middle East, and indicates that around 11,000 BCE an abrupt change to a drier, colder and more variable climate led to a steep fall in availability of the wild cereal crops that had long served as staples for hunter-gatherer communities. This period, which climatologists call the Younger Dryas (after a diagnostic flower which flourished in Europe at the time), corresponded to the first collapse of the Lake Agassiz ice dam, which led to a temporary reversal of the warming at the end of the last Ice Age. Some permanent hunter-gatherer villages were abandoned as resources and population declined, and first cultivation and later domestication of wild plants were developed to compensate. When, after a thousand years, the climate became warmer and wetter, an agricultural economy spread widely throughout the Middle East and beyond.[4]

From around 6200 BCE there was a 400-year global 'mini Ice Age' following the second great pulse of freshwater from the melting North American ice cap. There was drought in southeast Europe, Anatolia and the eastern Mediterranean, leading to the abandonment of many agricultural villages in the Middle East. There was also relatively rapid sea-level rise (on the order of 5cm a decade), causing large-scale migration and social disruption in low-lying and relatively flat areas such as the Persian Gulf and 'Doggerland', the highly productive region now covered by the North Sea.[5] (It was this sea-level rise that severed the land connection between what are now the British Isles and continental Europe.) But the most catastrophic result was the breaching of the barrier at the Bosphorus separating the Mediterranean from the fertile Euxine basin, creating the modern Black Sea. This permanently flooded more than 100,000km² within a couple of decades, and perhaps even in as short a time as two years – implying a local rise in sea level of up to 15cm *a day*. The displacement of population from this region may have been a significant factor in the spread of agriculture into central and western Europe.[6] The Younger Dryas event and the 6200 BCE event thus provide examples of both the impact of climate on human development on the broadest scale, and the sorts of non-linear impacts to be expected from global warming over the medium to long term.

After around 5000 BCE, global climate and sea levels had mostly stabilised, although there were still episodes of significant climate change at the regional and local levels. There were also continued but less severe global fluctuations. Six periods of rapid global climate change have been provisionally identified in the Holocene, corresponding to 7000–6000 BCE, 4000–3000 BCE, 2250–1850 BCE, 1550–550 BCE, 750–950 CE, and 1350–1800 CE. All but the most recent involved cooling at the poles, aridity at low latitudes, and major changes in atmospheric circulation and precipitation patterns.[7]

Despite regional warm episodes, it is unlikely that there were any periods over the last 10,000 years where global mean temperatures were warmer than the present, post-industrial warming.[8] However, less abrupt *warming trends* which peaked below current levels, following periods of global cooling, may have occurred. The most recent episode of rapid global climate change corresponds roughly to what has been termed the 'Little Ice Age' in Europe, and involved cooling at the poles but generally increased precipitation at low latitudes. Thus, even in periods of global climate change there was significant variation between and among localities and regions. Regional shifts in climate zones can also occur without major change in global averages.[9]

Environment, culture and conflict

Climate has been implicated in the collapse of many previous cultures, but there is a danger of putting the cart before the horse. As climate change has become intellectually fashionable over the last 30 years, the number of such attributions has multiplied. This has to a great extent been paralleled by an improvement in our understanding of paleoclimates stemming from the current research imperative behind global warming caused by human activity, but the data are often insufficient to deduce directly that climate was the cause of conflict or collapse. In most cases, the evidence is subject to interpretation, and there is not necessarily consensus or agreement in detail among period or regional specialists. It is only in the context of the consilience of evidence – ancient and modern, and across a wide geographical range and scale of complexity – that a coherent picture emerges.

During the mid-Holocene, climate change in different areas triggered cultural responses ranging from expansion to reorganisation to collapse; in some cases the same civilisation owed both its rise and fall to the vagaries of climate (see below).[10] But what we know about past climates improves in quality and detail the closer we get to the present day, as does the archaeological and historical record.[11] In fact, the relative stability of global climate after the mid-Holocene acts to some extent as a control against which individual cases can be interpreted; it brings into sharper relief the effects of climate change on societies and states and helps disaggregate climate from other factors contributing to instability and collapse.

Two cultures, two fates
The Polynesian islands of Rapa Nui (Easter Island) and the Pitcairn group some 2,100km to the west should be ideal laboratories to separate the various influences – including climate – on social and cultural development, decline or collapse. They are relatively or entirely isolated, and their social and political organisations were relatively simple. The most important developments are recent enough that adequate information should be available, yet they pre-date the first phase of globalisation in the eighteenth century, when European exploration and expansion began to influence or integrate such societies into a more complex network. But even in the absence of outside influences and complicating factors, it is not possible

to identify a simple cause, or chain of causes, for social and cultural developments. These cases demonstrate that even in such pristine conditions conflict has manifold, complex and interacting roots. They also offer a clearer insight into the dynamics of interaction.

Easter Island was settled before 900 CE, probably by a single expedition of Polynesians who had no subsequent contact with their home islands (or with anyone else, for that matter).[12] At its peak in the 1600s, the population had grown to around 15,000. It was divided into around a dozen clans, with some degree of social stratification between chieftains and commoners, but it was at least partially integrated religiously, economically and politically under a paramount chief. The geography of the island made this situation possible; other Polynesian islands with large populations tended to feature independent warring chieftaincies in each major valley.

When the settlers first arrived, the island had been heavily forested for millennia. A wide variety of tree and palm species, some up to 30m tall, provided food, fuel and raw material for buildings, boats and tools needed to erect the massive statues for which Easter is best known. Yet by the time that the first Europeans arrived in 1722, no trees over 3m survived. The evidence indicates that deforestation began as soon as the island was settled, peaked around 1400 and was essentially complete by the 1600s. Similarly, by 1500 most of the food sources – sea birds, pelagic fish, marine mammals, wild fruits – the settlers had relied on had disappeared or become inaccessible due to a combination of over-exploitation and the absence of wood for canoe construction. At the same time, crop yields also declined due to erosion and loss of shelter as a direct result of defor-estation. Construction of megalithic architecture and statues, which relied on labour fed by food surpluses, ended early in the 1600s. By the end of the century the population crashed, the complex traditional political and religious systems collapsed and were replaced by military coups and civil wars.

A similar story played out on Easter's similarly isolated nearest neighbours – a group of islands including Pitcairn and Henderson Islands, Mangareva, and some atolls unsuitable for permanent settlement. Settled around 800 CE, each of the three inhabited islands was deficient in some essential resources available on one of the others, and extensive network of trade and population-exchange between them flourished, connected through Mangareva with larger and richer islands 1,600km to the west. But by 1500, trade among the islands had ceased, and within a century or two Henderson and Pitcairn no longer sustained permanent populations. On Mangareva, as on Rapa Nui, environmental damage destroyed the economy and military coups overthrew the traditional order.

There is no direct evidence that changing climate was a factor in the environmentally induced collapses on either Easter Island or the Pitcairn island group. Pollen records, which show the variety and quality of vegetation at any given time, are often taken as proxies for climate, but, especially in such isolated cases, they can be misleading. The deforestation evident in the record was almost certainly the result of over-exploitation; a changing climate could well have narrowed the margin of error, but the error was human. Both collapses occurred soon after the rapid global climate change that precipitated Europe's Little Ice Age, when glaciers in New Zealand were growing and Chile experienced mostly wet, but highly variable, conditions.[13] Without local proxies, however, the direction and degree of climate change during this period in southeast Polynesia remains unknown. Like the megafauna that became extinct at the end of the last Ice Age, the forests had survived any number of similar climate-change events over preceding millennia; the new variable was human activity. If climate was a factor in the collapses, it was as an additional stress, not a primary driver. Finally, both Easter Island and the Pitcairn group are poorly endowed in other important geographical and environmental aspects compared to many other Polynesian islands.[14] In both cases, then, a combination of marginal environmental conditions, population exceeding resources, and inadequate adaptation to change all contributed to social collapse. A changing climate, if it played a role, was limited to narrowing the margin even further.

The interaction of climate and culture on another, much larger island on the other side of the world at around the same time offers a useful counterpoint. Between 985 and 1000 CE, two sheltered regions on the west coast of Greenland, separated by about 500km, were settled by Norse emigrants from Iceland, which itself had been settled between 870 and 930. The areas were uninhabited when the Norse arrived, although the colonists did find ruins left behind by Native American hunter-gatherers, who had lived in the area at various times over the previous three millennia, coming and going with their prey species in response to changing climate.

The Norse population grew to about 5,000 spread among about 250 farms. Although there was no formal hierarchy, the richest farmers in each settlement functioned as chieftains. Over the course of the next four centuries, the economy of Norse Greenland was based on subsistence agriculture and pastoralism, hunting and trapping. Infrequent voyages to Labrador provided timber, and there was only intermittent trade with Iceland and Europe. Nevertheless, the Norse Greenlanders were culturally European. They were Christians, with a bishop and a cathedral, monastery and nunnery (Eric the Red, who founded the settlement, was a pagan, but his son Leif built the first church in the New World; Iceland itself formally adopted Christianity in 1000 CE). They imported iron, lumber, tar and luxury items from Norway, and exported animal hides and furs, woollen cloth, and luxury items such as walrus ivory, gyrfalcons and even live polar bears. Their clothing fashions, burial customs and other cultural innovations tracked those of Norway.

Sometime before 1500 CE, the Norse settlements disappeared. The smaller, more marginal of the two failed some time before 1362; an expedition from the larger sent to help fight off encroaching Inuit found no one alive. Archaeological evidence suggests that, after a period of decline, the last inhabitants died of cold and starvation in a particularly bad spring. The last recorded contact with the surviving settlement was in 1406, when a Norwegian ship returned from Greenland to Bergen. The apparent causes of the decline and failure of the Greenland settlements are manifold: deforestation causing soil erosion and a shortage of fuel for smelting iron; over-exploitation of pastureland; hostile relations with the Inuit; the Black Death; and a decline in European demand for Greenlandic exports caused by that same plague, changing fashions and political conditions, and access to new sources of supply.

But unlike the Polynesian islands, in Greenland there is an abundance of direct evidence for climate change during this period. Cores from the Greenland ice cap are, in fact, among the best sources for prehistoric climate anywhere on the globe. The Arctic conditions mean archaeological evidence is well preserved, and there are contemporary historical records. In this case it is clear that worsening conditions due to climate change were a principal cause of the demise of the settlements, through both increasing the isolation of the colony from Iceland and continental Europe due to worsening sailing conditions, and through declining crop yields and prey species resulting in malnutrition and susceptibility to disease. The replacement

of the Norse settlers by a flourishing, unrelated Inuit culture
– with which they had long been in contact – moving down
from the north demonstrates, however, that survival in the
new conditions was possible, and suggests that cultural factors
led to an unwillingness on the part of the Norse Greenlanders
to adapt. Although there were certainly incidents of violent
conflict between Norse and Inuit, there is no evidence that
the replacement of the Norse by the Inuit involved deliberate conquest. Nor was it a question of resource competition,
since the two cultures did not rely on the same resources. And,
besides a cultural rigidity that made it difficult to adapt, there
was a cultural disposition among the Norse towards violent
dispute resolution, mediated by social mechanisms that broke
down under climate-induced stress.

The rise and fall of civilisations

These relatively recent and simple cases illustrate the difficulties involved in isolating the relative effects of climate change,
and provide a baseline against which to assess the response
of more complex civilisations, ancient and modern, to such
stresses. The period of rapid global climate change from 4000
to 3000 BCE involved a 'cool poles, dry tropics pattern', with
weakening of the monsoon system, increased rainfall variability and widespread aridification at lower latitudes.[15] This
led to the emergence of the first complex, highly organised
state-level societies in the central Sahara, Egypt, Mesopotamia,
the Indus Valley, northern China and Peru, as people clustered
around reliable sources of water and developed irrigation and
flood-control infrastructure.[16] Sumer, the first historical urban
civilisation, grew from a network of small settlements between
the Tigris and Euphrates rivers (in modern Iraq) from around
5,800 BCE at the end of the 400-year drought of the 'mini Ice
Age', as improving climatic conditions allowed a renaissance

of village-based agricultural and pastoral lifestyles. Even in the wetter climate beginning around this time, the fertile soils of the Tigris, Euphrates and Nile required intensive irrigation and flood-control measures, which the development of cities and increased social organisation allowed.[17]

When the climate turned colder and drier in the mid-fourth millennium BCE, with periodic drought, many cities in Mesopotamia collapsed under the stress, but others managed to adapt, increasing in size and complexity. By around 3100 BCE a true regional urban civilisation with extensive trade networks had emerged. It was unified politically into the world's first real state, the Akkadian Empire, around 2300 BCE, with trade links as far as Lebanon, Oman and Afghanistan. Yet after only a century, the northern half of the empire collapsed, with abandonment of many agricultural settlements in northern Mesopotamia and an influx of refugees in the south. A 180km defensive wall called 'Repeller of the Amorites' was built between the Tigris and Euphrates, near modern Falluja, to keep out the nomadic cultures that had replaced farmers and city dwellers in the north. The collapse coincided with the onset of a 300-year dry spell, and came despite a well-developed infrastructure designed as a buffer against large yearly variation in rainfall.[18]

At the same time, there was a reduction in flows down the Nile and failure of the annual flood due to decreased rainfall in equatorial Africa, leading to the downfall of the Egyptian Old Kingdom around 2150 BCE.[19] Although the evidence for climate-related social and cultural developments at this time is strongest for southwest Asia and Egypt,[20] it was a period of rapid climate change globally.[21] The Harrappan urban civilisation of the Indus Valley, in modern Pakistan and India, also ended abruptly around this time, coincident with a weakening of the south Asian monsoon and sharp reduction of precipitation in the Indus watershed.[22] As in Mesopotamia, urban civilisation in the Indus Valley probably emerged as a response to increasingly dry conditions after a long wet period that had allowed agriculture to flourish and spread.[23] There is evidence for similar climate-related transitions from complex to simpler societies in parts of China around this time as well, with drought in the north and flooding in the south.[24]

Archaeologists use the cultural transitions of c. 2200 BCE as the conventional break between the Early and Middle Bronze Ages in the Near East. Several centuries elapsed before complex societies began to be re-established in southwest Asia and North Africa. In some cases this happened before the 300-year drought ended; the internal unrest and independent warring provinces into which Egypt had dissolved were reunited in the Middle Kingdom in the mid-twenty-first century BCE. The end of the Middle Bronze Age around 1550 BCE is marked by the collapse of the Egyptian Middle Kingdom and of the Babylonian and the Assyrian Old Kingdoms, the successors to the Akkadians. Around 1200 BCE, the sophisticated international system of the Late Bronze Age, dominated by great powers (the Egyptian New Kingdom, the Hittite Empire in Anatolia, the Mycenaeans in the Aegean, the Mitanni in northern Mesopotamia, and Babylon in southern Mesopotamia) again collapsed, marking the end of the Bronze Age. Facing sustained drought and mass migration of populations from the north, known as the 'Sea Peoples', the various states and societies collapsed or retrenched, ushering in a 400-year 'dark age'.[25]

The rapid climate change in southwest Asia and the eastern Mediterranean at the end of the Bronze Age was part of a repeating pattern. Europe's climate is characterised by three dynamically interacting climate regimes, which are reflected in the characteristic distribution of plant and animal species. The maritime climate regime, which currently encompasses Britain, most of western Europe (including northern Spain and Italy), Scandinavia and a broad swathe of northern Russia, is cool and wet in summer and mild in winter. The continental regime, which encompasses eastern Europe, the northern Balkans, southern Sweden and Finland, and most of Russia, Belarus and Ukraine, is warm and wet in summer and cold and dry in winter. The Mediterranean regime, which encompasses most of Iberia, Italy, the southern Balkans, the Mediterranean coasts of France, Croatia and North Africa, and extending to the Middle East, is characterised by hot, dry summers and mild, wet winters.

These climate zones are determined by global atmospheric circulation patterns and the position of major air masses, which in turn determine the weather. Unusual heat waves or cold snaps are often the result of a temporary shift of these air masses. But the boundary between the northern maritime/continental regimes and the southern Mediterranean/Sahelian regimes has lain more than 600km north or south of its current position at different times over last three millennia. Between around 1200 and 300 BCE, Spain, Italy, the Balkans and Anatolia featured maritime or continental climates, while between around 300 BCE and 300 CE most of Europe, with the exception of Britain and Scandinavia, was in the Mediterranean zone.[26] The rapid climate change around 1200 BCE was associated with a southern shift in the zonal boundary, associated with drops in mean temperature of around 2–3°C in the eastern Mediterranean.[27]

The period 300 BCE–300 CE roughly coincides with the rise and extended domination of Rome. Over the course of about 350 years, from the middle of the fourth century BCE, Rome's hegemony and rule expanded from a small part of central Italy to encompass the entire Mediterranean. By the end of the republic in 19 BCE the empire had reached, with minor exceptions, the frontiers it would maintain for the next 400 years. Since

Rome's rivals enjoyed the same climate, it could not explain the emergence of the world's most complex economic, political and social organisation, but it may have been a necessary precondition. The fall of Rome, though, is another story. Since the empire's economy relied on expropriation of wealth from conquered territories, once it reached the natural limits of its expansion it faced a chronic fiscal crisis and began to feed on itself. Social and political institutions became increasingly ossified. Its collapse was probably inevitable, even if the climate had stayed benign.[28] But when the climate shifted, Rome's northern provinces were weakened at the same time that drought on the Central Asian steppe led to large-scale migrations of tribes, leading to the 'barbarian' invasions that ultimately conquered all of the western empire. A similar chain of events had taken place from the ninth to the fourth century BCE, when Celtic tribes overran northern Italy and even sacked Rome.[29]

It is notable that the eastern Roman empire (Byzantium) survived the collapse in the west; it faced less pressure from migrating tribes, had a more robust economic system and was organised along a different social pattern.[30] But the long-term climate shift, coupled with a sudden but short-lived global climate shock in 536–537 CE due to a major volcanic eruption (probably in Southeast Asia), weakened the Eastern Empire. The 536 CE eruption caused widespread crop failure, and may have contributed to the Plague of Justinian in 542 CE (perhaps the first outbreak of bubonic plague in Europe) that devastated the Byzantine Empire. The geopolitical consequences were profound: the weakening of Byzantium and the Persians, the Romans' neighbours and rivals, removed the major barrier to the explosion of Islam out of the Arabian peninsula after the death of Mohammed in 632 CE.[31]

The next bubonic plague pandemic, the Black Death of fourteenth-century Europe, followed a similar period of better-than-average climate known as the Medieval Warm Period or Little Climatic Optimum, from around 1000–1300 CE. Because much early work on historical climate was based on data from Europe and the North Atlantic, this period was long thought to have been unusually warm throughout the globe. More recent work suggests, however, that although average summer temperatures in northern and western Europe in this period may have been as much as 1°C above twentieth-century averages, the warming was most likely limited to the northern hemisphere, or even to parts of Europe, and the start and end points of the Medieval Warm Period as identified by proxies such as pollen or tree rings vary by decades from place to place.[32] Nevertheless, this period saw the economic and cultural flowering of the High Middle Ages, when population and land under cultivation reached levels they would not see again until the sixteenth or seventeenth century, and the cultural and political boundaries of the West were extended into central Europe, the Iberian Peninsula, the Middle East (through the Crusades) and the North Atlantic. From the thirteenth century average temperatures began to return to the long-term mean, but with a high degree of variability. The expanding European population and economy had reached its natural limits by around 1300, and remained fairly stable, with perhaps some decline, until the advent of the Black Death and subsequent crash.[33]

The pattern of high climate variability from decade to decade in Europe that followed the Medieval Warm Period led into the Little Ice Age, which corresponded with the most recent of the six periods of global rapid climate change in the Holocene. Like the end of the Climatic Optimum, it is impossible to date the advent of the Little Ice Age precisely, since it was not a period of sustained colder temperatures but rather one in which the long-term average was brought down by more frequent extremely cold years (or sequences of years), and an increased frequency of extreme events. Thus, it could be considered to have begun as early as 1300 or as late as 1500. But, however defined, the start of this cooler period corresponded with the decline and collapse of the Norse Greenland settlements, the internal contraction of settlement in Europe, periodic epidemics of the plague, dropping crop yields, an increase in the frequency and extent of warfare, and profound cultural changes including religious persecutions and witch hunts – but also the roots of the scientific and industrial revolutions. Though a multitude of devils may be lurking in the details, it would not be wrong to say that many of the broad political, economic, social and intellectual developments that define the end of the Middle Ages and the rise of the modern global order – including Westphalian states, enlightenment liberalism and capitalism – were in part adaptations to the changing climate.[34]

Climate played an important role in the course of Chinese civilisation, and the lucky coincidence of two millennia of detailed historical and climate records makes China an ideal laboratory. A fine-grained, 1,810-year reconstruction of precipitation patterns in northern China reveals that changes in the Asian monsoon correlate with both Chinese temperatures and cultural changes, as well as with solar variability and with climate and cultural events elsewhere, such as the European Medieval Warm Period and Little Ice Age and the collapse of Mayan culture in Central America. The end of the Tang (618–907 CE), Yuan (1271–1368) and Ming (1368–1644) dynasties each came a few decades after an abrupt shift to weaker monsoons and drought, while the flourishing of the Northern Song dynasty (960–1127) coincided with a monsoon peak.[35]

Over the last 1,000 years, population growth in China has been sensitive to changes in average temperature on the scale of decades, but has been mediated by regional geography, the imperfect correlation between temperature and precipitation fluctuations, and social factors.[36] The broad pattern of warfare, too, correlates with climate change over the last millennium, and was certainly a factor in the population fluctuations. The same pattern of drought on the steppe that led to the barbarian attacks on Rome was at work in East Asia as well. Famine and nationwide uprisings tended to occur during cold phases. Outbreaks of warfare tended to lag climate change due to social buffers; both the frequency of warfare and the lag with climate change vary between north and south. The temperature anomaly in China over this period tended to vary by only 0.5°C above or below the norm, though there was a warming peak of around 1°C around 1250 and a cooling of more than 1°C in around 1644, coinciding with the fall of the Ming dynasty. Extreme climate conditions in northern China during this period, which corresponds to the worst of the Little Ice Age in Europe, led the Manchus to attack the Ming Empire, which had been weakened by half a century of drought, flooding, famine, disease and pest outbreaks, and peasant revolts.[37]

In the New World, too, climate fluctuations tend to correlate with the archaeological record of cultural changes – in coastal and highland Peru, the American Southwest and California, the Great Plains and Central America.[38] There are, to be sure, examples of the collapse of complex cultures, especially in Central America, for which there is no evidence that climate was a factor. But there is insufficient evidence to implicate other factors either. On the other hand, Central America provides one of the best and most fully investigated examples of prehistoric cultural collapse: the Mayan civilisation that flourished in parts of modern Mexico, Guatemala, Belize and Honduras in the first millennium CE. In some respects the Maya represent an ideal example, illustrating a range of responses to climate change in varying circumstances within a single culture. The culture encompassed three ecological zones and experienced three extended droughts corresponding to different phases of the civilisation. Small, sedentary farming communities relying on slash-and-burn agriculture began to emerge in the Mayan homeland in the second millennium BCE, under the influence of earlier cultures to the north. Large stone buildings appeared around 500 BCE and the first large ceremonial centres about a century later. Development continued despite an extended drought from 475–250 BCE, since the population was still relatively small and dispersed and agricultural techniques were flexible enough to cope. A second drought from 125 BCE–210 CE led to abandonment of large ceremonial centres and dispersal of the population. The Classic Mayan Period dates to around 250 CE, with the first written evidence for the emergence of dynasties or kingdoms. The population and the number, scale and complexity of monuments and buildings continued to increase steadily until the early eighth century CE. At its peak, the population density in the Mayan homeland was far higher than it is today. However, a period of decreased rainfall lasting from around 750–1025 CE, and containing four episodes of more severe drought, coincided with the collapse of the civilisation. In the richest ecological zone, the southern lowlands, the population declined by more than 99%. There was more continuity in the northern lowlands, where the population had access to groundwater resources, but the political-religious system broke down there as well. Other factors certainly contributed to the collapse, including warfare and over-exploitation of resources, but climate change was almost certainly the major driver.[39]

Modern times

All the examples cited above pre-date the age of European global exploration, expansion and colonisation. The modern age is usually said to begin just before 1500 CE, with the discovery of the New World, the invention of moveable type, and the fall of Constantinople to the cannon of the Turks – all Eurocentric metrics. Although the collapse of southeastern Polynesian cultures and the Ming dynasty in China came in the seventeenth century, it was nevertheless before they came into significant, if any, contact with Western civilisation. The global expansion of European hegemony provides a unique case – the clash of pre-industrial and proto-industrial cultures – for analysis of cultural collapse and instability for reasons other than climate change. Later cultural and social developments, in the context of an increasingly global and industrialising system from the second half of the eighteenth century onwards, provide clearer examples of both climate- and non-climate-related instability and collapse.

The discovery and settlement of the New World and the essential replacement of the aboriginal population by Europeans was the most profound cultural development of modern times. It led initially to the collapse through military conquest of the Incan Empire in Peru and the Aztec Empire in Mexico, due to European political and technological supe-riority stemming ultimately from the fortuitous, favourable circumstances of Eurasia's ecology and resource base.[40] Both conquests were aided by the deaths of significant portions of the native population, and important leaders, from diseases, especially smallpox, carried by the newcomers. Other advanced New World societies collapsed in the face of such epidemics even before they came into regular contact with Europeans, as well as by military action and direct infection.

While estimates vary widely and data are almost impossible to come by, a native population on the order of 50m in both hemispheres, the bulk in the Incan and Aztec Empires, declined by 80–95% in the first century or so after contact.[41] This popu-lation crash, representing about 20% of the global population, led to massive regrowth of forests, which removed enough CO_2

from the atmosphere between 1500 and 1700 to have been a significant cause of the Little Ice Age.[42] Reforestation in Europe following the Black Death a few centuries earlier may also have contributed to the cooling.[43]

While prehistoric, pre-modern and early-modern examples provide insight into the dynamics of climate, conflict and collapse, cases from the twentieth century are perhaps more directly relevant to assessing future threats, since the economic, social and political conditions are more salient. Many Americans fail to realise, for example, that America itself experienced significant climate-induced social disruption during the Dust Bowl of the 1930s.

A series of annual droughts (1930–1931, 1934, 1936, and 1939–1940) in the American West, particularly the Great Plains, combined to create the worst sustained period of drought in the region for over 200 years. It contributed significantly to the depth and prolongation of the Great Depression, led to the migration of over 2m people, and cost perhaps as much as $1bn (more than $15bn in today's terms) in federal relief payments.[44] Although there has been a pattern of cyclic drought in the American West, correlated with La Niña events, stretching back for over 2,000 years, as well as periods of severe drought lasting for centuries, the Dust Bowl was unusual in its geographic pattern of temperature anomalies as well as in the extensive dust storms which lent it its name. Its severity was due to changes in land use: the conversion of the more drought-resistant prairie to wheat farming, and subsequent crop failure and soil erosion, turned the topsoil into dust. The storms that carried this dust across much of the continent in turn amplified the drought.[45]

Perhaps the most geopolitically salient collapse of modern times has been the disintegration of the USSR. Why the Soviet system collapsed in 1991 has been the subject of many books, including a deluge in 2009 on the 20th anniversary of the fall of the Berlin Wall. Despite, or perhaps because of, the vast amount of documentary evidence, the question is more complex and more difficult than that of the fall of Rome. But setting aside the difficulty of defining what collapse means in this context, as perceived at the time or in the not-yet mature verdict of history, the general consensus is that the fall of the USSR stemmed from the inability of an inefficient command-economy structure to cope with the demands of the arms race, increased consumer demand due to exposure to the West, social pressures from the Helsinki Accords, and fallout (figuratively and literally) from the Chernobyl nuclear reactor accident in 1986.[46] Likewise, the break-up of Yugoslavia, made possible in part by the Soviet collapse, was driven by economic crises, external pressure, latent ethnic tensions, nationalism and contingent political factors. To some small extent the Soviet collapse can be blamed on the weather: an inefficient agricultural system made the country particularly vulnerable to extreme weather events. But weather is not climate. No individual event can ever be definitively attributed to climate change, and there is nothing in the case of the USSR to suggest that the droughts were outside the range of expected variation.

The failure or collapse of states in the developing world, too, has become increasingly salient geopolitically over the last 30 years or so. The reasons for such failures, to be discussed in the next chapter, have been manifold, and in most cases appear to have been unrelated to climate, although the example of Sudan and the conflict in Darfur, to be examined later, is particularly instructive.

The lessons of history

In his 2005 book *Collapse*, Jared Diamond set out to examine why and how different societies failed or adapted in the face of specifically ecological and environmental disasters. His comparative approach, which examined southeastern Polynesia, Greenland and the Maya as well as other examples such as the Anasazi in the American Southwest, the New Guinea highlands, Tokugawa Japan, and modern Rwanda, Haiti, China, Australia and Montana, was thus uninterested in cases of collapse where environmental factors were not significant. He did, however, acknowledge there were no cases in which a society's collapse could be solely attributed to such factors, and identified four further categories of possible contributing factors beyond self-inflicted environmental damage: hostile neighbours, friendly trade partners, the society's response to environmental crises, and climate change. Of these, he isolated the willingness or ability of a society to respond appropriately as the only factor that was always significant.[47]

Turning this around to answer the question of how climate change contributes to instability, conflict or collapse is revealing, and in this context some of Diamond's comparative case studies are particularly so. He shows that the ethnic strife and genocide in Rwanda in the mid-1990s was not simply motivated by historical tensions or cynical politicians, but was a Malthusian worst-case scenario, where population growth simply outstripped resources.[48] The outcome was not predetermined, but the demographic and ecological trends were in this case necessary (albeit not sufficient) conditions for the conflict. Diamond offers Haiti and the Dominican Republic as contrasting examples: they share a common environment (the large Caribbean island Hispaniola) but their fates could scarcely have been more different, so Haiti's chronic weakness and environmental degradation can be attributed primarily to cultural causes.[49] Finally, the periodic collapses, reorganisations and abandonments experienced by societies of the American Southwest in 1100–1500 CE exemplify multiple proximate

environmental causes and cultural responses, but were all ultimately due to the same fundamental challenge of living in a
difficult environment, where successful short-run solutions
failed or created fatal problems in the long run, in the face of
unanticipated natural or man-made environmental changes.[50]

There is little or no evidence of warfare or violent conflict in
the Paleolithic; it was only when population densities began to
rise and permanent settlements were established, giving rise
to competition over resources, territory and perhaps ethnic
difference, that violent conflict became widespread. The rise
of complex hierarchical societies made it commonplace.[51] But
agriculture, population growth, permanent settlements and
increasing social and technological complexity were all adaptations to climate change.[52] Drought, famine and rising sea levels
led to conflict at least as much through spurring migrations
of peoples – another form of adaptation – as through direct
impacts on societies.[53] Over the five millennia from the end of
the last Ice Age to around 5,000 years ago the evidence reveals a
range of cultural responses to climate change, from collapse to
reorganisation to expansion, although some important cultural
changes do appear unrelated to climate.[54]

The extended drought around 3200–3000 BCE in
Mesopotamia, for example, led to increased cultural sophistication and complexity, urbanisation and expansion and the
emergence of Sumerian civilisation, while the drought a thousand years later at the end of the Early Bronze Age around 2200
BCE saw the collapse of the Akkadian Empire. The cultural
responses to similar climate changes differed in Mesopotamia,
Egypt and the Sahara in the mid-Holocene. In the Sahara, a
humid phase following the end of the Ice Age allowed the
spread of semi-permanent settlements of hunter-gatherers,
who turned to cattle pastoralism as the climate again became
increasingly arid. As desiccation continued two divergent

trends emerged: replacement of cattle by sheep and goats and a more mobile pastoral culture; and increasing sedentarism, territorialism, urbanisation and social complexity, with more intensive exploitation of local resources.[55] Eastern Saharan pastoralists abandoned the nomadic lifestyle and settled in the Nile Valley. In Mesopotamia, urbanisation and the development of more complex societies began earlier than in the Sahara or Egypt. By 3200 BCE distinct regional cultures were already beginning to emerge, before the emergence of Sumerian civilisation in the south. In the Nile Valley, in contrast, this period saw the unification of Lower and Upper Egypt after a period of regionalism and interacting proto-states.[56] The same range of responses to the abrupt climate change around 2200 BCE – imperial collapse, habitat-tracking and lifestyle changes, and migration – is evident throughout the Mediterranean, southwest Asia and the Indus Valley.[57] Climate change was a factor in the crises of civilisation in southwest Asia at the end of the Early and Late Bronze Ages (2200 and 1200 BCE), but not for those at the end of the Middle Bronze Age (1550 BCE).

Urbanisation and increased social and economic complexity as adaptive responses to climate change ultimately increase vulnerability to such change, as societies rely on more and more complex systems and technology. Increased complexity means increased fragility, as well as more severe consequences when systems finally fail, a dynamic evident in the collapse of Easter Island and the Mayans, among others. In the modern world, the wealthier industrial nations are much more resilient to climate or other shocks (whether environmental or not) than pre-industrial societies or less developed countries, but if they do reach the breaking point the collapse will be further and faster. This applies to economic and social systems as well as physical infrastructure, as the global financial crisis of 2008–2009 demonstrates. But besides increasing vulnerability, social and economic responses to climate change can also impose cultural constraints on further adaptation. Loss of mobility is a simple example. Hunter-gatherers settle in permanent locations in response to climate change either as an adaptation to drought or because a benign climate means more bountiful resources and little need to move. But once in permanent settlements, they can no longer simply follow food sources in response to climate-induced changes in supply, without significant social disruption.[58]

This raises, once again, the question of what 'collapse' actually means. The collapse of the Indus Valley civilisation, for example, was at least initially not a full-blown collapse but a process of adaptation through de-urbanisation and changing agricultural practices, with a high degree of cultural continuity in other respects.[59] Whether Harrappan civilisation was destroyed by a changing climate is a semantic question. Its society was unique among ancient civilisations – despite large urban centres, it was not characterised by high economic and social stratification or centralised state power.[60] In this respect it was the exception that proves the rule. To borrow a term from evolutionary biology, it was pre-adapted to cope with a changing climate.

Cultural attributes of mobility and flexibility can similarly pre-adapt a society; in effect, adaptation is part of the cultural toolkit. In the southwestern United States, for example, the Anasazi and Chaco Canyon cultures responded to extended droughts by abandoning urbanised settlements; there were large-scale movements of peoples, but these took place within established kinship networks, without evidence of violent conflict.[61] They were, in effect, migrants rather than refugees. But this only works where there is space, where the alternative resources are not already under the control of or contested by another group. Finally, one culture's fall can be another's

rise, as, for example when climate shifts allowed an expanding Rome to replace Celtic polities in Gaul and elsewhere. One
culture can be better adapted to particular climatic or ecological
conditions, such as the Inuit culture that expanded southwards
at the time the Norse colony in Greenland collapsed. In any
case, in modern times, with a global population an order of
magnitude higher than in the pre-industrial period, adaptation
through internal and external migration will create its own
problems for security and stability.[62]

There are other cultural, political or social barriers to adaptation and mitigation. One is the tragedy of the commons,
where individuals acting in their own immediate interests act
collectively against the interests of society. This is a particular
problem of egalitarian and democratic societies; authoritarian
systems have a greater capability to impose solutions for the
collective good, although perhaps less inclination – authorities too often act in their own selfish interests at the expense
of society as a whole.[63] People are not always rational actors:
cultural values may make them reluctant to abandon unsustainable lifestyles. The Norse Greenlanders kept to their traditions
rather than adopt aspects of Inuit lifestyle that proved successful in the changed environment, and they paid the ultimate
price.[64] Communist rule survived in China but failed in Russia,
because the Chinese Communist Party let its system develop
into a form of state capitalism while the Russians were unwill-
ing to abandon their ideology. In the end, of course, Russia
turned to a similar path as China, but only after a systemic
collapse and break-up. Other traits that can lead to individuals or societies failing to address problems that ultimately lead
to conflict or collapse include a tendency to think in the short
term, either out of immediate survival needs or due to the
cycles imposed by particular political systems, or tendencies to
groupthink or denial.[65]

The ability to adapt thus depends not only on physical capacity but on cultural willingness. The drought that created the Dust Bowl in the 1930s, for example, was worse than a similar drought that occurred in the same region in the 1890s, but the impact in human terms was not as severe. In the nineteenth century the agricultural economy of the Great Plains was not fully integrated into the national economy; the farmers had less sophisticated technical capabilities to cope with drought; and no support was available from the national government. The result was depopulation on a scale much greater than in the 1930s. Resilience was even greater during a similar drought in the 1950s, when improved technology and state and federal assistance programmes adopted in response to the Dust Bowl meant there was no net migration.[66]

Finally, the distinction between weather and climate, too, becomes important in the context of social collapse. A society poised at the tipping point can be pushed over by a natural disaster, whether a one-off extreme weather event or a geophysical catastrophe. A major volcanic eruption on Iceland around 1159 BCE may have led to a period of increased warfare and a 50% reduction in population in Bronze Age Scotland.[67] A less severe eruption of a different volcano in 1783 led to the deaths of 50% of Iceland's livestock (including 80% of its sheep) and up to 25% of the population. It caused thousands of deaths in Europe through atmospheric pollution and weather effects, and its climatic impact lasted for a decade, contributing to a series of famines that helped trigger the French Revolution.[68] An even smaller eruption in 1875 devastated the Icelandic economy and, along with a series of unusually cold summers and stormy winters, led to the emigration of 20% of the population to North America – an option that had not really been available before.[69]

Extreme weather events have also been implicated in the outcome of military campaigns, wars and elections.[70] The

George W. Bush administration's inadequate response to the devastation caused by Hurricanes Rita and Katrina in 2005 was an important factor in the recent leftward shift in American politics. Climate change will make extreme weather events more frequent and more severe, and add to the underlying stress that might make a non-climate factor more likely to push a society past the tipping point. While the deterioration of conditions in Norse Greenland was due to climate change, for example, it was an extreme cold snap that put the final nail in the coffin for the first of the settlements to disappear. On the other hand, many of the civilisations of antiquity developed in response to the need to cope with such one-off shocks, and only collapsed after sustained periods of drought.

Critics of the idea that anthropogenic climate change poses a threat to the stability or cohesion of modern societies and nations have rightly pointed out that historical and pre-historical cases of collapse or disruption where climate has been a factor all resulted from one-off or cyclical cooling phases, not warming.[71] This tendency is exemplified by the cyclic nature of climate and warfare in China over the last millennium.[72] But global mean temperature is likely already higher than it was for any of these cases, and the current and projected rate of further warming is also unprecedented. Twenty-first-century climate change starts from a high baseline and takes us into uncharted territory, so the historical precedent that collapse tends to be induced by cooling episodes is far less relevant than the precedent that societies are indeed sensitive to changes in climate. It is not the mean temperature that is important, moreover, but rather the global or regional consequences in terms of rainfall and seasonal temperatures. Drought has been the main culprit in past climate-induced collapse during periods of cooling, but increased frequency and severity of drought is also a projected consequence of anthropogenic global warming. Although precipitation patterns are among the least robust of projected consequences, with the greatest variation between and among climate models, overall the twenty-first century is expected to be increasingly warmer and wetter, and in places, too wet. But other regions – even if they cannot be identified with any certainty – will be too dry. Past climate–culture interaction is, however, not necessarily predictive of future performance.

Changes in mean global temperature in whatever direction result in widely variable regional and even local impacts. The Medieval Warm Period saw an expansion in Europe but a series of societal collapses in the western hemisphere. The cooler, wetter conditions that caused chaos in Europe during the Little Ice Age were a boon to societies in arid regions such as Central Asia.[73] From a global, long-term perspective, however, there is a broad correlation between periods of rapid climate change and social and cultural developments.

The findings with regard to climate change, war and population decline in China discussed earlier in this chapter have been replicated for Europe during the Little Ice Age. A suggested explanation for this correlation between climate and conflict is that the available social mechanisms for adaptation to climate change and ecological stress in Europe at the time were inadequate. Migration was limited by established political boundaries and often resulted in war; economic change involving cultures, technologies and habits was often too costly and slow to avoid famine and disease; trade and redistribution were inadequate in the face of regional or global crises; and international and national institutions were not sufficiently developed to buffer the tensions arising from food insecurity.[74] More recent work focused on Europe found a weaker correlation between climate change and violent conflict over the last millennium, and noted that the link becomes even weaker in the post-industrial period.[75]

The degree to which climate influences history, and more specifically the degree to which climate change affects stability, conflict and collapse, remains contentious. Experts immersed in the details of particular cultures or periods often see more proximate factors as being of greater import. But if the question is not which peculiar circumstances or dynamics of a given society may have led to its contraction or demise, but rather what commonalities can be discerned across a range of such events, climate emerges as a key (albeit not universal) contributing factor. This is not surprising, given that all cultures ultimately depend on basic food and water resources, which are sensitive to climate change. It is clear that climate change does not always lead to contraction or collapse, and that contraction or collapse can occur in the absence of climate change. But climate cannot be ignored, since instances of climate change have challenged cultures throughout history. The way they met that challenge as much as the nature of the challenge itself provides a mirror for the security challenges posed by unprecedented warming we now face.

CHAPTER THREE

Darfur: The First Modern Climate-Change Conflict

The violence in the Sudanese province of Darfur is the largest and latest in a series of sporadic conflicts going back to the 1980s, originating in tribal competition over access to grazing land and water.[1] Fighting broke out in February 2003 when a new rebel group, the Sudan Liberation Army, launched attacks on local police stations. By 2007 over two million people had been displaced, many fleeing across the border to Chad, and the number of killed and wounded has been estimated by the United Nations at somewhere between 200,000 and 500,000.[2] In June of that year, UN Secretary-General Ban Ki-moon ignited a widespread debate when he declared that human-induced climate change was an important contributing factor to the Darfur conflict[3] – a point previously argued by a number of commentators, including former Vice President Gore in *An Inconvenient Truth* in 2006.[4] On the eve of the UN Security Council debate on climate change and security in April 2007, the UK's Special Representative for Climate Change John Ashton said 'the security implications of climate changes are bigger than we thought even two or three years ago. Their effects can already be seen in Darfur.'[5] At the end of 2008, the number of internally displaced persons had reached 2.7m, and over 250,000 had fled to neighbouring countries.[6] Fighting continued, despite ongoing peace talks and the presence of a 19,000-strong United Nations–African Union peacekeeping mission. Bad governance was undoubtedly a particularly important contributor to the conflict and to the failure of peace efforts. It also hindered international humanitarian relief operations. However, with regard to its onset and severity, the fighting in Darfur can accurately be labelled the first modern climate-change conflict.

Geographical, cultural and ecological contexts

Modern Darfur is the westernmost state of the Republic of the Sudan, for the most part a semi-arid plain lying between the Nile basin and Lake Chad. It can be considered part of the Sahel, the ecological region stretching across Africa from Senegal to Eritrea and representing the transition between the Sahara Desert to the north and the more humid savannah to the south. Rainfall in the northern parts of Darfur, which primarily support camel-herding nomads, averages only around 300mm a year, while a semi-humid belt in the south and southwest can receive around three times as much, and supports commercial agriculture and cattle-herding nomads. In between lies a higher-relief, semi-fertile area supporting subsistence agriculture.

The population of Darfur is, in Gérard Prunier's words, a 'complex ethnic mosaic', with over 36 main tribes speaking Arabic and various African languages. Many of the tribes found in Darfur also live elsewhere in Sudan and in neighbouring countries such as Chad and the Central African Republic.[7] The modern Sudanese distinction between 'Arab' and 'African', often viewed as the basic divide in the contemporary conflict, is an ideological, cultural construction dating from the middle of the twentieth century rather than a reflection of ethnicity or historical origins.[8]

Darfur: ecological, cultural and conflict zones.

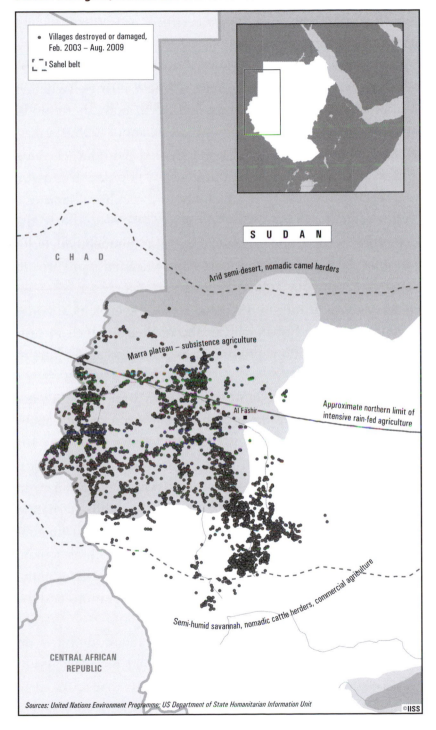

- Villages destroyed or damaged, Feb. 2003 – Aug. 2009
- Sahel belt

SUDAN

CHAD

Arid semi-desert, nomadic camel herders

Marra plateau – subsistence agriculture

Al Fashir

Approximate northern limit of intensive rain-fed agriculture

Semi-humid savannah, nomadic cattle herders, commercial agriculture

CENTRAL AFRICAN REPUBLIC

Sources: United Nations Environment Programme; US Department of State Humanitarian Information Unit

©IISS

The complex ethnic distinctions in Darfur are perhaps less important than the contrast between agriculturalists and pastoralists. The relationship between the two is governed by competition for land and water resources, which can be affected by short- and long-term climate change (whether random, cyclical or greenhouse-induced), both in terms of absolute availability and geographical extent of the resources. Historically, the two lifestyles coexisted without clashing and in fact functioned symbiotically. But population growth, together with declining productivity of agricultural land due to low rainfall and increasing losses to pests, necessitated the expansion of land under cultivation. A simultaneous deterioration of pastureland meant pastoralists needed more area to support a growing animal population.[9] Moreover, changes in the level of aridity in the Sahel cause the ecological zones to shift southward or northward accordingly, which in turn affects the competition between pastoralism and agriculture in a given area.

The climates of the Sahel and Sahara were much wetter than the present from the end of the last Ice Age until about 5,000–6,000 years ago. A weakening of the monsoon led ultimately to desertification of the Sahara and more arid conditions in the Sahel, which led to the advent of pastoralism in the region.[10] These arid conditions persisted, with alternating drier or wetter periods on a scale of centuries, and fluctuation of the ecological zone boundaries by as much as 300km. Such episodic shifts had a noticeable impact on societies in the region, causing famines and contributing to migrations and the growth and collapse of states.[11]

After a particularly wet episode in the 1950s, there was an extended period of desiccation in the Sahel from the 1960s to the 1990s, with severe drought in the early 1970s and early to mid-1980s. Darfur in particular experienced a very severe drought in 1980–1984, and again in 1990.[12] In the 1990s a trend towards wetter conditions in the Sahel began, and in 2003 there was especially abundant rainfall, causing flooding and landslides in parts of the region.[13] Exceptionally wet conditions, with rainfall about 15% above average of the previous 55 years, or 60% above the average for 1971–2000, occurred again in 2005.[14] It will be decades before it becomes clear whether this represents a significant shift back to a wetter climate or is simply a random fluctuation. Some models of greenhouse-induced climate change do forecast wetter conditions for the Sahel, but others do not, and there is no consensus on the matter.[15] There is some evidence that the decline in rainfall in the second half of the twentieth century was not gradual; indeed one analysis of rainfall data points to a sudden change in the early 1970s from a period of relatively stable, wetter conditions (1940–1972) to drier but similarly stable conditions (1972–2002).[16] Whether or not this is the case, rainfall remains below long-term norms, with 2005 a particularly bad year and 2007 the worst in over a decade.[17] Paradoxically, the health and vigour of vegetation in Darfur has increased since 2003 despite the drought. In a cruel irony, the fighting, and subsequent depopulation and reductions in livestock, eased ecological stress in some areas.[18]

History of the conflict

The United Nations Environmental Programme (UNEP) reported in 2007 that 29 of the 40 violent local conflicts in Darfur since independence in 1956 involved grazing and water rights.[19] Until 1970, such conflicts were mostly resolved locally through established structures, but since then legal reforms have destroyed such mechanisms without providing a viable alternative.[20] After Jaafar al-Nimeiry came to power in a military coup in 1969, his regime, made up of pan-Arabists,

Ba'athists, communist sympathisers and independent intellectuals, ended indirect and chiefly rule and dismantled local native courts, replacing a centuries-old system with one that never really worked.[21] Movement of pastoralists from Chad who do not respect the traditional conflict-resolution mechanisms is also a factor.[22] An influx of small arms into the region has also made conflicts more violent and difficult to contain.[23] These developments weakened the ability of society to cope with the stresses placed on it by a more arid climate.

In 1983 the Sudan People's Liberation Army/Movement (SPLA/M) under John Garang initiated a civil war in largely Christian southern Sudan in response to the introduction of sharia law and retraction of the limited autonomy the south had won in 1972. In 1987 the Khartoum government began arming Arabic-speaking Muslim pastoralists in southern Darfur against the putative threat from the south.[24] This followed the severe drought of 1980–1984 in Darfur, which culminated in the famine of 1984–1985 that caused widespread displacement of peoples, conflict between pastoralists and farmers, and 95,000 deaths.[25] Following a further famine in 1990, the SPLA/M made incursions into Darfur, where it was defeated by government forces and local Arab militias (precursors of the modern Janjaweed) in 1991–1992. The militias then turned against a number of non-Arab tribes, who reacted by forming armed militias of their own.[26] Low-intensity conflict continued until 1999, and there were sporadic outbreaks of political violence up to the resumption of major conflict in February 2003.[27]

The Darfur rebel groups blamed the Islamist and Arab-centric regime of President Omar al-Bashir, which came to power in a coup in 1989, for oppressing and displacing African farmers in favour of Arab pastoralists. The government responded to the 2003 attacks by training and arming militia groups and sending troops for counter-insurgency. Fighting between militia groups, and between the rebels and government forces, spread, and there were widespread reports of atrocities against civilians.

A UN-brokered peace agreement in 2006 was accepted by some, but not all, of the rebel groups. Violence continued despite an African Union peacekeeping mission from 2004 and a joint UN–African Union mission from 2007, a failed ceasefire and renewed peace talks. By the beginning of 2010, however, the full-scale fighting seemed to have dampened down into a low-intensity conflict. Some displaced persons even returned to their homes to plant crops for the first time since 2003, but the situation remained fragile and unpredictable.

Climate and causality

The question of whether, and how much, climate change contributed to the conflict in Darfur has become a focal point in the wider debate about climate change and security. To many, the coincidence of drought and conflict makes the causal link self-evident. On the other hand, an empirical study of correlation between rainfall patterns and conflict in Darfur and the wider Sahel seems to suggest that, rather than a steady decline in average annual rainfall, there was a major shift around 1971, with relatively stable patterns in the 30-year periods before and after; a similar pattern occurred in other Sahelian countries. As part of the study, an examination of 38 African countries, 22 of which showed such structural breaks in rainfall, found no obvious relationship between such breaks and later conflict, leading the authors to reject the argument 'that Darfur's conflict is best thought of as a climate change conflict'.[28] However, a more recent empirical study covering all of sub-Saharan Africa between 1980 and 2002 showed a strong correlation between annual temperature variations and the incidence of civil war.

This finding held true when controlled for a range of data sets, models and variables, including precipitation, per capita income and degree of democracy.[29]

What these and similar studies show is that climate change is neither necessary nor sufficient to cause conflict. But as discussed in Chapter 1, two different questions are being asked, both generally and in specific country cases. The first is: 'what causes conflict?' This entails an examination of the relative contributions of different factors, and whether they are deterministic or predictive. The second is: 'does climate change cause conflict?' It asks whether, other things being equal, climate change increases the risk or severity of conflict.

It is incorrect to view these questions as synonymous, or to see the second as subsumed in the first, as would be the case if it were a simple question of environmental determinism. For even if climate change is neither necessary nor sufficient to cause conflict, there can nevertheless be cases where it does contribute through exacerbating other risk factors. This lies at the core of the concept of climate change as an exacerbating factor or threat multiplier. For example, John Ashton said on the eve of the April 2007 Security Council debate on climate and security that the Darfur conflict was an early sign of the sorts of threats that would arise as a result of global warming:

> Like most conflicts, it's complex. It results from an interplay of a lot of social and political and possibly ethnic factors. But there is absolutely no doubt that it's a more difficult conflict to deal with, because on top of all that, you've had a 40-percent fall in the rainfall in northern Darfur over the last 25 to 30 years, again in a way that's entirely consistent with what the climate models would have told you to expect.[30]

The 2007 report by analysts from the CNA Corporation which introduced the concept of climate as a threat multiplier into the policy debate, argued that 'Darfur provides a case study of how existing marginal situations can be exacerbated beyond the tipping point by climate-related factors'.[31] These factors do not need to be specifically resource-related. For example, drought in the 1970s and 1980s contributed indirectly to another Sahelian conflict, the Tuareg Rebellion in northern Mali in 1990–95. Young men were forced to migrate to neighbouring Algeria and Libya, where many were radicalised. Meanwhile, embezzlement of international drought-relief funds by state officials was contributing to popular unrest. The drought was probably not a necessary condition for the outbreak of rebellion, which was not driven by supply-induced scarcity.[32] Nevertheless, the example shows how climate can interact with contingent social and political factors to multiply their impact.

Looking at the correlation of climate change and conflict in Darfur in greater detail reveals that such an interaction of factors is indeed at work. Firstly, even if average annual rainfall in the Sahel, and Darfur in particular, did not decline steadily but dropped abruptly, there was still significant variation from year to year within the two periods before and after 1971 which seem to show flat trends. It is this very variability that makes identifying the long-term trend and whether it is gradual or abrupt so problematic. Such short-term fluctuations can contribute to environmental stress and conflict, especially since they appear to have become more frequent and more severe since the late 1980s.[33] Although the trend suggests the droughts of 1980–1984 and 1990 'did not provoke widespread conflict',[34] 15 of the 29 local conflicts in Darfur over grazing and water rights identified by UNEP since 1956 occurred in the periods 1980–1984 and 1990–1991.[35]

   Alex de Waal's detailed analysis of the causal chain is revealing.[36] Firstly, he argues that, although the immediate cause of
the 1984–1985 famine was the severe drought of the early 1980s,
a causal relationship between man-made climate change and
the drought has not been proven. Drought and environmental degradation led to shortages of food, but only because of a
lack of economic development and because the inhabitants had
no opportunity to use the available resources more efficiently.
Since the population at the time of the 1984–1985 famine was
only around half what it was before the outbreak of large-scale
violence in 2003, de Waal argues, the earlier famine was not the
result of population outstripping resources, but rather due to
a lack of infrastructure and available investment for fertilisers
and irrigation; 'the food crisis only led to famine because of
governmental neglect'.
   The aftermath of the famine and the measures the inhabitants
took to cope was impoverishment and social breakdown, but
de Waal argues that the violence that broke out was not a spontaneous response but a result of deliberate government policy,
the influx of weapons from Libya and Chad, and the presence of
a predatory Chadian militia, which gave many young, impov-
erished men the opportunity to engage in organised violence.
This was coupled, as a result of internal migration, economic
reconfiguration and declining faith in government, with an
acceleration of the decline of traditional community authority
that began in 1970 when the sultanate system and local tribal
administrative apparatus was formally abolished.[37]
   Migration and changes in livelihood created unprecedented
'actual and latent disputes that later became the focus of armed
conflict', but significant violence only erupted because of political factors, 'particularly the propensity of the Sudan government
to respond to local problems by supporting militia groups as
proxies to suppress any signs of resistance'. Drought, famine

and their consequences only made it easier to pursue this strategy. De Waal thus argues that 'the most important culprit for violence in Darfur is the government, which not only failed to utilise local and central institutions to address the problems of environmental stress in Darfur, but actually worsened the situation through its militarised, crisis management interventions whenever political disputes have arisen'.

The observation that the link between global warming and the famine is unproven is trivial, since climate scientists agree that only patterns and trends, and not specific weather events or anomalies, can be positively attributed to climate change caused by human activity. But there is strong evidence for human-induced changes in the Sahel over the last 30 years, which are entirely consistent with the predictions of the computer models.

Contributory factors to the climate conditions of the last five decades include land degradation from local human activity, such as overgrazing and deforestation; changes in global temperature patterns; and various feedback mechanisms. The relative contributions of local and external factors, including greenhouse-induced global warming, are unclear. It is also unclear whether the recent conditions are historically unprecedented. Moreover, whether the observed climate change in Darfur can be attributed to human activity is not critical to the argument that climate was a contributing factor to the violence. The best explanation for the recent dry episode is, however, changes in atmospheric circulation stemming from warming of the Indian Ocean, which is consistent with greenhouse-induced global warming.[38] The decline in precipitation in the Sahel over the twentieth century was greater than in any other region.[39]

The rest of de Waal's analysis reveals a textbook example of multiple and complex causation. In a subsequent exchange with him, Thomas Homer-Dixon argues that commentators' and researchers' implicit assumption that multiple causes are additive is where much of the discussion on Darfur as a climate crisis runs aground. Complex causation suggests that the various causes are multiplicative or interactive, so that one cannot hypothetically change or subtract a single factor such as climate change to see what happens. 'Such mental manipulations almost always produce erroneous and even meaningless results ... Changing one thing will have ramifying and unpredictable consequences through the entire causal network ... It's pointless to ask about, or to argue over, the *relative* importance of climate change as a cause of the violence'.[40] Homer-Dixon points out that most of de Waal's analysis 'seems to implicitly acknowledge not only multicausality but also the impossibility of discriminating among the relative power of causes'. Calling the Sudanese government 'the most important culprit for violence' is therefore unsupportable.[41] De Waal defends his conclusion through a reductionist argument that does not directly address Homer-Dixon's point. He compares environmental conditions and the timing and severity of violence in sub-regions in Darfur and Sudan, and concludes: 'there's an empirical consistency of link between the militarization of government authority and conflict, which just isn't there for environmental or climatic change and conflict'.[42] This is true as far as it goes, but merely exemplifies the point that what is meant by causation depends on why the question is asked.

A contrasting illustration is provided by UNEP's analysis of conflict and the environment in the Sudan. In this case, the authors are primarily interested in the specific environmental aspects of recovery, reconstruction and development, and they explicitly exclude other factors to focus on the environmental dimensions of conflict.[43] Like de Waal, they note that environmental problems affecting pasture and farmland occur throughout Sudan and are 'clearly and strongly linked to conflict in a minority of cases and regions only', but that never-theless 'there is substantial evidence of a strong link between the recent occurrence of local conflict and environmental degradation ... in the drier parts of Sudan'.[44] Like de Waal, they discuss the breakdown of traditional systems of mediation and dispute resolution after 1970 and the influx of small arms into the region, 'with the unfortunate result that local conflicts today are both much more violent and more difficult to contain and mediate'.[45] Although they also recognise that land degra-dation 'does not appear to be the dominant causative factor in local conflicts', they conclude that:

> There is a very strong link between land degrada-tion, desertification and conflict in Darfur. Northern Darfur – where exponential population growth and related environmental stress have created the condi-tions for conflicts to be triggered and sustained by political, tribal or ethnic differences – can be consid-ered a tragic example of the social breakdown that can result from ecological collapse. Long-term peace in the region will not be possible unless these underly-ing and closely linked environmental and livelihood issues are resolved.[46]

The preceding analyses suggest there is no real disagreement that the Darfur conflict is in some sense an environmental conflict, merely a difference of emphasis and perspective. It was not caused by climate change, if 'cause' is meant as both a necessary and sufficient condition. But in the case of Darfur, it is clear that the further one gets from a simplistic, reduction-ist view of causality the more climate change (and probably greenhouse-induced climate change) is a critical factor under-lying the violence. To the extent that the question of climate change as a security issue is paramount, to say that other factors were equally, or even more, important politically or morally is not to deny that Darfur was a climate-change conflict.

CHAPTER FOUR

Conflict, Instability and State Failure: The Climate Factor

Although state failure and collapse have been present throughout history, they became increasingly salient for the global order in the post-war era. Their importance has continued to increase with the end of the Cold War and the rise of global terrorist networks, as epitomised by Somalia and Afghanistan in the last two decades. The 2002 National Security Strategy of the United States noted for the first time that weak states posed as great a danger to the national interest as strong states, and the 2006 Strategy stressed the importance of prevention or resolution of regional conflicts – regardless of cause – that could lead to state failure, humanitarian crises and creation of safe havens for terrorists, and for intervention and post-conflict stabilisation and reconstruction to avoid such outcomes.[1] This was recognition that failed states pose sufficient direct and severe security threats to justify a significant commitment of resources toward preventing them. With climate change potentially contributing to regional conflict and state failure, understanding its role can help choose between policies intended to reduce or avoid such risks.

The failure of governance in Sudan long preceded the current Darfur conflict. It was one reason why the fighting broke out and was able to spread and continue for so long. Yet the violence in Darfur began just as the long civil war in the south came to a negotiated end, raising hopes for renewed nation-building and development. This raises the question: how representative is the Darfur conflict of how changing climate might interact with other factors affecting state stability over the next few decades?

Why states fail

With the proliferation of new states – the 'Group of 77' developing states now has 130 members – and an increasingly interconnected world, state failure has risen as an international concern. The world has more stable states than ever before, but also more weak or fragile states. Many of the new states created in the wave of decolonisation after the Second World War and after the end of the Cold War lack historical traditions, established institutions, developed economies and adequate resource bases. Failure threatens global stability because it can lead to increasing violence, both criminal and political; loss of control over borders and parts of national territory; increased ethnic hostility; and migration to neighbouring countries with their own stability issues or to developed countries.

As in the historical cases of social and cultural collapse discussed earlier, the causes of state failure can be geographical, physical, historical or political, and contingent and idiosyncratic human decisions can be as important as structural or institutional weaknesses. Signs of impending failure can include rapidly deteriorating living standards, shortages of foreign exchange, corruption, subversion of democratic norms, breakdown of civil-society and most state institutions and expansion of security institutions, and ethnic tensions. In a vicious cycle, the state begins to provide fewer and fewer services to its citizens until, ultimately, state legitimacy crumbles. The outcome is variously civil war, break-up, or total collapse, as in the case of Lebanon in the 1980s, Sierra Leone in the 1990s or Somalia in the last decade.[2]

A weak state is not necessarily a failing one; a failing state will not inevitably fail; and a failed state will not inevitably collapse. In 2002 political scientist Robert Rotberg identified one collapsed state (Somalia) and seven (Afghanistan, Angola, Burundi, the Democratic Republic of the Congo (DRC), Liberia, Sierra Leone and Sudan) as states that could be characterised as failed for at least the preceding decade. Other failed states, such as Lebanon, Bosnia, Tajikistan and Nigeria, had recovered from failure. He argued that there were perhaps two dozen failing states, including Colombia, Sri Lanka, Indonesia and Zimbabwe, while many more could be considered weak.[3] A variety of measures have been developed to identify, characterise and categorise weak, fragile or failed states, including the Fund for Peace/*Foreign Policy* Failed States Index (FSI); the Brookings Institution's Index of State Weakness in the Developing World (ISW); and the Country Indicators for Foreign Policy project at Carleton University (CIFP). These indices use different indicators (from 12 to 83, each in turn based on many more underlying variables) and different algorithms for weighting and grouping. The different methodologies produce strikingly divergent results (see Table 1). Although there is some degree of overlap, only ten states appear among the top 20 in all three lists.[4] The profound disagreement between these models for assessing state fragility, not to mention those that purport to predict conflict, violence or state failure,[5] is an indication that the dynamics are almost certainly too complicated, and at the very least insufficiently understood, to lend themselves to this sort of empirical analysis. This, incidentally, contrasts with the relative agreement of climate models across a range of complexity, inclusion and initial conditions in projecting climate change.

Table 1. **The 20 most fragile states (by average rank in three indices)**

	CIFP 2008	FSI 2009	ISW 2008
Somalia	4	1	1
Sudan	1	3	6
Afghanistan	2	7	2
DRC	3	5	3
Iraq	6	6	4
Haiti	8	12	12
Côte d'Ivoire	12	11	10
CAR	20	8	7
Burundi	7	24	5
Chad	16	4	16
Zimbabwe	26	2	8
Ethiopia	5	16	19
Pakistan	9	10	33
Liberia	10	34	9
Myanmar	23	13	17
Nigeria	14	15	28
Guinea	27	9	23
Nepal	13	25	22
Eritrea	11	36	14
Yemen	15	18	30

The examples of pre-industrial human civilisation and the modern conflict in Darfur show that societies and polities fail, disintegrate or collapse due to a complex interaction of environmental, political and economic circumstances and trends. Of these, unfavourable environmental conditions, and particularly climate, are perhaps the most basic and direct, but are not necessary companions to failure. While a society's willingness and ability to adapt based on social, cultural and institutional structures, as well as the actions of individual actors, are paramount, some adaptive mechanisms, such as migration, expropriation, and transformation to simpler or more complex forms of organisation, can themselves lead to conflict within the society or between it and its neighbours. In his seminal work on the collapse of complex societies, anthropologist Joseph

Tainter attempted to distil these various factors and mechanisms – he identified 11 distinct, sometimes contradictory but often overlapping, approaches to explaining such collapses – within an overarching, unified framework. The factors include resource depletion or over-abundance, extreme environmental events, inability to respond to change, external rivals, intruding populations, internal contradictions and conflict, social dysfunction, mystical factors, contingent events, and economic explanations. Climate change falls under the rubric of resource depletion, which subsumes both gradual deterioration of a resource base due to mismanagement and rapid loss due to environmental (particularly climatic) fluctuations. Tainter argues that while none of these (besides the mystical explanations) is without merit, none goes far enough. His preferred explanation, elaborated in some detail, essentially boils down to the law of diminishing returns:

> At some point in the evolution of a society, continued investment in complexity as a problem-solving strategy yields a declining marginal return ... Ultimately, the society either disintegrates as localised entities break away, or it is so weakened that it is toppled militarily, often with very little resistance. In either case, sociopolitical organisation is reduced to the level that can be sustained by local resources.[6]

Tainter claims this theory has the capacity to incorporate the various other explanatory themes he identified – themes which also emerged from the examples in the previous chapters. For example, he argues that a major weakness of the resource-depletion theme does not explain 'why resource stress leads to collapse in one case and economic intensification in another'. His explanation is that 'if the marginal utility of further economic development is too low, and/or if a society is already economically weakened by a low marginal return, then collapse in such instances would be understandable. Collapse is not understandable, under resource stress, without reference to characteristics of the society, most particularly its position on a marginal return curve.'[7] Similar arguments apply to other environmental, social, political or economic explanations of collapse. Tainter's theory thus offers a framework in which to integrate the various factors in a situation of complex and multiple causation, to assess their relative weights as ultimate and proximate causal factors. It is at this level that the more abstract measures of aggregate impact of climate change – as a percentage of global GDP, or in terms of the 'social cost of carbon' – are most relevant.[8]

The framework, however, is incomplete or misleading in two important respects. Firstly, as Jared Diamond, who is concerned specifically with environmentally induced collapse, has pointed out, Tainter's reasoning assumes that complex societies, like the members of those societies, are rational actors, and therefore suggests they are not likely to 'allow themselves to collapse through failure to manage their environmental resources'.[9] Setting aside the assumption that individuals are always rational actors, it is clear from the preceding chapters that complex societies are not. Cultural, political and social barriers can and do intervene to prevent adaptation to changing conditions.

Secondly, Tainter argues that the dynamics underlying the collapse of complex societies before globalisation and industrialisation no longer apply, because 'the world today is full'. Societies can only collapse in a power vacuum, he argues, but for the first time in history there is now no place on Earth unoccupied by a complex society.[10] But historical analogies are still valuable:

Past collapses ... occurred among two kinds of international political situations: isolated, dominant states,
and clusters of peer polities. The isolated, dominant
state went out with the advent of global travel and
communications, and what remains now are competitive peer polities. Even if today there are only two
major peers [he was writing in 1988] ... the dynamics
of the competitive relations are the same. Peer polities, such as post-Roman Europe, ancient Greece and
Italy, Warring States China, and the Mayan cities, are
characterized by competitive relations, jockeying for
position, alliance formation and dissolution, territorial
expansion and retrenchment, and continual investment in military advantage ... Although industrial
society (especially the United States) is sometimes
likened in popular thought to ancient Rome, a closer
analogy would be with the Myceneans or the Maya ...
Collapse, if and when it comes again, will this time be
global. No longer can any individual nation collapse.
World civilization will disintegrate as a whole.[11]

Any such global collapse, even given current unsustainable
trends in consumption, population and development, the
increasing fragility that comes with complexity, and the threat
of climate catastrophe, is not on the immediate horizon. And
while Tainter's argument may well hold true for the world as a
whole over the long term, in the short term it is clearly belied by
the existence of failed states. Tainter argued that in the modern
world such states 'would not be allowed to collapse, but will
be bailed out either by a dominant partner or by an international financing agency'.[12] The difference is one of perspective:
over a decade or more, a failed state may well be revived and
reconstituted through outside intervention; this is certainly a

major international policy goal. But states still fail, and this is a critical concern from the point of view of security experts and policy planners, not to mention those who live in such states. The bridge between the two perspectives is this: short-term state failure, disintegration or collapse, and subsequent inter-vention and reconstruction, is a catastrophe for those directly involved, a security threat for other states, but an adaptation mechanism for the global system.

Taking these two caveats into account, then, Tainter's theory can put the role of climate change in state failure or collapse into perspective. States fail when they reach the point of dimin-ishing returns, but where this point lies in a particular case depends as much on social, political and cultural factors that enhance or inhibit a given society's ability to react as it does on economic truths. The environmental impacts of climate change are only one small input into this complex dynamic system, but even small inputs can have huge consequences as they ramify throughout the system. No particular input can be privileged over any other, either in theoretical terms or in specific cases. Rotberg's claim that 'state failure is man-made, not merely accidental nor – fundamentally – caused geographically, environmentally or externally'[13] – essentially the same claim that is made for those who de-emphasise the climate factor in the Darfur conflict – is a valid moral judge-ment, but not the basis for prioritising policy responses in one arena over those in another.

The climate factor

Despite the lack of agreement among various models or indices of state failure, the various categories, metrics and indicators they use offers a way in to the problem of iden-tifying how climate change might affect the risk of violence, instability, failure and collapse in different countries and regions. Only four of the nine indicators (out of a total of 83) grouped in the environmental category in the CIFP – arable/fertile land availability, disaster risk index, renewable water availability, deforestation – will, for example, directly change as a consequence of climate change. Neither the ISW nor the FSI include explicit environmental indicators, but two of the 20 indicators in the ISW, access to water and improved sanitation and undernourishment, will indirectly reflect climate change. Since none of the indicators, moreover, are really independent – a change in any one will percolate throughout the system – climate change will affect most of the others indirectly, albeit some more directly than others. Refugees produced or hosted, migration and income inequality, for example, should all be expected to vary directly with climate, although the degree to which they do so will be affected by other factors related to state capacity or resilience. The same is true of indicators where the connection to climate is more tenuous, for example public health or economic growth. Finally conflict extent, nature and intensity are considered as indicators of fragility in some of the models. If the question is whether and how climate change will affect these factors, they should be considered more as consequences than as causes, even taking into account the irreducible interdependence of the various factors within a complex dynamic system.

Globally, warming is expected to reduce the availability of clean, fresh water. Total precipitation will probably increase, but the pattern will not be uniform: there will be higher precipitation at high latitudes and lower precipitation in subtropical land regions. The seasonal pattern of precipitation will change, and even in regions where overall rainfall is expected to decrease, the number of heavy rainfall events will rise. Besides this increase in the frequency of extreme events, there will be an increase in the overall variability of precipitation seasonally and annually, and the overall rise in precipitation will take longer than the warming trend to manifest against this increased natural variability. Higher water temperatures, changes in rainfall intensity and increased variability in flows will exacerbate pollution, affecting ecosystems, human health and reliability of water systems. The net overall impact of climate change on water availability will be negative in all regions, even those where total precipitation is expected to increase, because of the increased annual variability, seasonal changes, water quality and flood risks.[14] Reduced availability will not just affect water for drinking and food production: water is critical in many industrial processes, especially energy production, and a significant amount of energy goes into water treatment and extraction.[15]

In 1990 only five countries in Africa suffered from water scarcity. By 2025, even without taking climate change into account, Egypt, Somalia and South Africa are expected to join them because of population growth and development, and a further 12 countries – Mauritius, Lesotho, Ethiopia, Zimbabwe, Tanzania, Burkina Faso, Mozambique, Ghana, Togo, Nigeria, Uganda and Madagascar – will experience water stress.[16] Climate change is expected to exacerbate this, especially in northern and southern Africa. In eastern and western Africa there will probably be a net reduction in water stress by mid-century, albeit with some populations at increased risk.[17] In Latin America the net number of people experiencing water stress due to climate change is likely to increase by 7–77m by the 2020s.[18] Peru and Colombia are particularly vulnerable over this period due to reliance on glacier run-off, which is expected to decline drastically. This will also severely affect hydro-electricity generation.[19] In Asia, 0.12–1.2 billion people are projected to experience increased water stress by the 2020s.[20] Even if overall precipitation increases, changes in the seasonal pattern can still mean there is a risk of water shortages, and this can be exacerbated by melting glaciers. For example, the maximum monthly flow of the Mekong River, which drains much of Cambodia, Vietnam, Laos, Myanmar and southwest China, is projected to increase by 35% in the basin and 16% in the delta in 2010–2038 compared to 1961–1990, but the minimum flow will decrease by 17% and 24% respectively. Thus there may be an increased risk of flooding in the wet season, and water shortages in the dry.[21]

The impact of reduced water availability on food production will be substantial, but climate change will affect food security in other ways, such as changing the length of the growing season, increasing the frequency of extreme weather events, changing the prevalence of crop pests and diseases, and through CO_2 fertilisation (where the increased concentrations of CO_2 in the atmosphere contribute to increased crop yields). Globally, the potential for food production is expected to increase in the short term, with large regional variations: crop productivity will increase slightly at mid- to high latitudes, but decrease at lower latitudes, especially in arid and tropical regions with dry seasons.[22] The projected number of people at risk of hunger depends strongly on the choice of emissions scenario, even if the climate impacts are comparable, since the scenarios make different assumptions about both population growth and socio-economic development, including prices and income levels.

Since these assumed demographic and socio-economic trends would lead to an overall reduction in malnourishment by as much as 80% by the end of the century in the absence of climate change, only the worst-case emissions scenarios show net rather than relative increases in food scarcity.[23] From a baseline of 854m undernourished in developing countries in 2000, for example, estimates of the number at risk in 2020 are

630m and 782m for two scenarios, and climate change alters these by +1.6–4.8% to 640–660m and -0.6 to +2.9% to 777–805m respectively.[24] Thus while climate change increases the total number of people at risk, this number will still be lower than the 2000 baseline, since it is assumed that economic growth will be a rising tide that raises all boats. Similarly, for example, the number of people expected globally to suffer increased water stress by 2025 varies from 395–1,661m according to scenario, despite similar climate projections. Perhaps surprisingly, the scenario with the greatest humanitarian impact in 2055 is not the one that shows the greatest climate change.[25]

Beyond the question of food availability, climate change will affect food security through stability of supply, access to resources by individuals or groups, and food safety, quality and storage. These factors, which create a negative feedback, are not taken into account in the population and development assumptions built in to the scenarios, which could mean the projections for impacts on food availability are underestimated. In the next few decades, the overall impact of climate change on food production may be low compared to other impacts, but so will the degree of socio-economic development that would ultimately shield the poorest populations from such impacts.[26] The regions where food security is currently low are characterised by a subsistence economy and local markets, making the populations particularly vulnerable, although a projected increase in dependence on food imports for developing countries will bring its own problems.[27] The ecological impacts of climate change will have further effects on food availability and forestry, with both economic and environmental consequences. Deforestation both accelerates climate change by removing one mechanism that removes CO_2 from the atmosphere and exacerbates food and water impacts by changing run-off patterns and increasing soil erosion. Coastal wetlands and coral reefs, both of which support important fisheries, will be negatively affected on balance, as will other marine ecosystems.[28]

Crop yields from rain-fed agriculture in some countries in Africa could decline by 50% by 2020, with increased risk of crop failure and high livestock mortality, especially in eastern and southern Africa.[29] Projected impacts on crop yields in Latin America are sensitive to choice of emissions scenario as well as to CO_2 effects, but the net increase in people at risk of hunger here is likely to be 1–5m by 2020.[30] More temperate countries such as Argentina and Uruguay could even see improvements in agricultural and pasture productivity over the short term.[31] In Asia crop yields could decrease by 2.5–10% in the 2020s compared to 1990, and the number of people at risk of hunger or malnutrition could be 7–14% higher than baseline projections in the same period.[32] Projections to 2030 suggest that South Asia and southern Africa stand out as regions with large numbers of people expected to suffer food insecurity without sufficient adaptation measures. They do so, however, only because the projections for annual or seasonal changes in precipitation are strongly negative across all models used, while changes in precipitation for other regions, particularly eastern and western Africa, the Sahel and west Asia, are much more uncertain.[33]

One aspect of the impact of global warming on coastal ecosystems will be the increased frequency and severity of storms, exacerbated by sea-level rise. Other extreme weather events, such as heatwaves and cold snaps, will also affect societies beyond their impacts on food and water security. In contrast to the more common pattern where climate change is expected to affect lower-latitude countries, which tend to be poorer, disproportionately, the effect of more frequent and severe summer heatwaves will be particularly felt in mid-latitudes in the northern hemisphere, especially in urban areas in the northeastern United States, China, Japan and Europe; witness the August 2003 European heat wave which caused up to 35,000 premature deaths. In areas such as South Asia, the Middle East or North Africa, where the highest temperatures normally come in the dry season, and the average temperatures are higher, societies are pre-adapted to cope with such extreme events.[34] Temperature extremes have impacts beyond human health, including increased demand for energy for heating or cooling, and for water; crop failures; and impacts on food and water storage and other infrastructure. Extreme events such as tropical cyclones, storm surges, heavy precipitation, flooding and drought will have similar effects as well as affecting tourism, erosion, settlement and migration, and causing other economic damage.[35] Globally, despite improvements in forecasting and disaster relief, droughts and floods remain the greatest current weather-related threats.[36]

Does climate matter?

The aggregate systemic impact of climate is notoriously difficult to measure or project. Estimates of the social cost of carbon – that is, the economic value of the marginal impact of emitted carbon – range, for example, from $1 to $1,500 per tonne; the wide range stems in part from the uncertainties in climate science discussed earlier, but mostly from different subjective judgements about discount rate, treatment of equity, monetisation of non-economic impacts and likelihood of catastrophic impacts.[37] The net costs, moreover, in some places or among particular groups of people will be significantly higher than the global average due to regional differences in warming, different regional climate responses to global warming, high sensitivity to impacts or low adaptive capacity.[38]

A study designed to avoid some of the problems and uncertainties underlying previous aggregate approaches recently looked at annual variations in temperature, precipitation and economic output in countries around the world from 1950–2003. Higher temperatures substantially reduced both the rate and amount of economic growth in poor, but not rich, countries. Poor countries experienced, on average, a decline in growth by 1.1 percentage points for each 1°C rise in temperature in a given year. These correlations were evident – and even stronger – for increases in temperature over a decade or longer, suggesting that poorer countries have been, on average, unable to adapt to the negative consequences of climate fluctuations over that time scale. Higher temperatures reduced both agricultural and industrial output, investment, innovation and political stability. Assuming poor countries would nevertheless adapt to the impact of a given increase in temperature after ten years, the impact on growth would still be large. Since the results suggest that the economies of rich countries are relatively insensitive to climate fluctuations, the result would be a widening gap between rich and poor. There was also a correlation between higher temperatures and political instability.[39]

Such correlations do not assume or demonstrate any particular underlying mechanism. They are in keeping, however, with what would be expected from theories of state failure. The risk factors or drivers, moreover, for state failure that are directly related to climate and those that are not are not independent of one another. The same factors of geographical position or barriers that limit access to markets, for example, can also increase exposure to climate change. The most important secondary impact of climate change driven by the primary impacts on water and food security, ecosystems impacts, extreme weather events and sea-level rise is likely to be large-scale migration or population displacement. Within developing countries, poor farmers will on average see their income drop, both in real terms and relative to wealthier sectors, in the next few decades.

Migration is usually an option of last resort, and those driven to such measures are often those least able to afford them. Most migration will thus be from rural to urban areas, and within the worst-affected nations and countries rather than from such regions to developed nations.[40]

Adaptation to climate impacts is not entirely a function of national conditions – other things being equal, individual choices can make a significant difference at the local level. In the face of drought, for example, residents of one village in Gujarat, India, have recently made collective efforts to build water storage facilities, irrigation systems, and barriers to slow run-off. They manage three harvests a year. Residents of a neighbouring village who have made no similar efforts grow a single crop and are dependent on the government to truck in drinking water for most of the year.[41] But, in general, poorer communities and nations, especially those experiencing rapid urbanisation, tend both to depend more on climate-sensitive resources and to be less able to afford or attempt adaptation measures. Democratic and civil-society institutions tend to be weaker in poorer countries, and autocratic or corrupt governments also less likely to even try to implement such measures.

Health status and level of education as well as governance and accountability are predictive of resiliency to climate impacts.[42] Bangladesh, considered highly vulnerable to rising sea levels and increasingly violent storms, has nevertheless recently seen a drop in typhoon deaths, while neighbouring Myanmar has seen an increase. The difference is the willingness of the two governments to invest in warning systems and resiliency, and to accept foreign assistance.[43] Pre-adaptation in the form of resiliency and infrastructure is particularly important for coping with increased variability and extremes, since any social system will have a threshold beyond which it will be unable to cope – 'the worst matters much more than the bad'.[44]

Climate change is already altering the distribution of some infectious disease vectors, and this is expected to continue. Where robust public health systems already exist, the net impact of these changes will be negligible. However, where such infrastructure is lacking, or is particularly vulnerable, changes in human or animal disease patterns could cause significant disruption beyond a simple increase in mortality or morbidity. In 1873, for example, the United States entered a six-year economic depression in part because of a pandemic of equine flu which crippled a horse-dependent transportation system.[45] No economy is now quite so dependent on animals for power or even food, but countries that rely on large-scale export of a single crop or grow a limited range of high-yield or genetically modified varieties are at particular risk, especially as such monocultures are often adopted in response to pre-existing food insecurity.[46]

The worst climate-change impacts on countries such as Saudi Arabia and the Gulf states may not be water or food shortages, but relative reductions in revenues if the consumption of oil declines in response to emission-reduction efforts. For example, global oil consumption is projected to increase by 24% between 2008 and 2030 assuming business as usual, but by less than 5% if countries collectively adopt policies that would limit CO_2 concentrations to levels assumed to avoid dangerous climate change (see Chapter 5).[47] Without adequate adaptation funding, in the form of aid from the developed world, climate-change mitigation could have as much impact on some states as climate change itself in the short to medium term – the cure may be as bad as the disease.

Finally, the complex interactions between climate change, economic, social and political variables, and conflict and instability create feedbacks that amplify climate impacts. Conflict and state failure make adaptation to and mitigation of climate change more difficult, as state institutions become less able to implement adaptation measures and international non-governmental organisations are unable to operate safely, as in Darfur.

Three variables affect whether a particular state is at an increased risk of failure due to climate change: the degree of exposure to specific physical impacts, the sensitivity of the economy or society to those impacts, and the ability (capability and willingness) to adapt.[48] In the short to medium term nothing can be done about the physical impacts. Reducing sensitivity to climate-change impacts is of course possible, but that is, by definition, adaptation. Analysis of both pre-modern social and cultural responses to climate change and concepts of state failure indicates that adaptive capacity is the crucial variable.

Fragile states can be divided into two groups: those where the principal drivers or risk factors for failure are not directly related to climate, and those where there is a direct connection. States in the first group may be affected by climate change simply by the addition of a new stress and by the fact that the risk factors they already exhibit (poor governance, for example) make it harder to adapt. The second group may be pushed towards failure or even over the edge by a relatively small degree of climate change; although they presumably have some capacity to cope with such stresses, this capacity may already be stretched to the breaking point. Countries where both aspects are important, but which belong properly to the second category, are obviously the most vulnerable to climate change, although they are also the most vulnerable to changes in non-climate-related factors. Sudan epitomises such states.

Although it is tempting to take various metrics, indices and rankings of fragile states, or of aggregate climate impacts, at face value to inform policy, their inherent weaknesses limit their usefulness, and in fact may make their use counter-productive. There is a coarse correspondence between various rankings of fragile states, which parallels the conventional wisdom informed by expert, qualitative judgements, but the lack of correlation in detail suggests they add little value to such judgements. Taken together, however, such indicators can help identify states or regions which merit particular and detailed attention.

It is also important to distinguish among fragile states – between, for example, weak, failing, failed or collapsed states – as the relative importance of climate change may differ, all other things being equal. States on or beyond the verge of collapse are already of great concern to their neighbours, other states with interests in the region, and the wider international community. Although climate change will make such states more vulnerable, their very fragility makes the shock of extreme events within the normal year-on-year climate variability a greater risk than the systemic effects of climate change. Climate change may be a factor in the next few decades in pushing states from failure to collapse, or from failing to failed, but it is not likely to be a particularly significant one, as such states tend to be weak across the board and sensitive to influences unrelated to climate. The real differential impact of climate change will be on stronger, but still fragile, states, nudging them off the path of development and reversing attempts at recovery and reconstitution.

States of concern

Since the characteristics that make states or societies suscep-tible to failure or collapse tend to overlap with those that affect the capacity to adapt to a changing climate, the assumption that climate change is a simple threat multiplier is reasonable. But although fragility is an important contributory factor to

State fragility and vulnerability to climate change

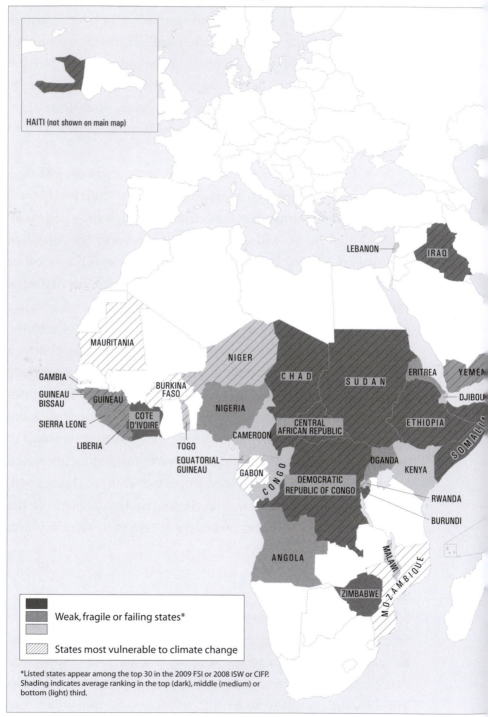

HAITI (not shown on main map)

LEBANON

IRAQ

MAURITANIA

NIGER

GAMBIA

BURKINA FASO

CHAD

SUDAN

ERITREA

YEMEN

GUINEA BISSAU

GUINEA

NIGERIA

DJIBOU

SIERRA LEONE

COTE D'IVOIRE

CENTRAL AFRICAN REPUBLIC

ETHIOPIA

LIBERIA

CAMEROON

SOMALIA

TOGO

EQUATORIAL GUINEA

GABON

CONGO

UGANDA

KENYA

DEMOCRATIC REPUBLIC OF CONGO

RWANDA

BURUNDI

ANGOLA

MALAWI

MOZAMBIQUE

ZIMBABWE

■ Weak, fragile or failing states*

▨ States most vulnerable to climate change

*Listed states appear among the top 30 in the 2009 FSI or 2008 ISW or CIFP.
Shading indicates average ranking in the top (dark), middle (medium) or
bottom (light) third.

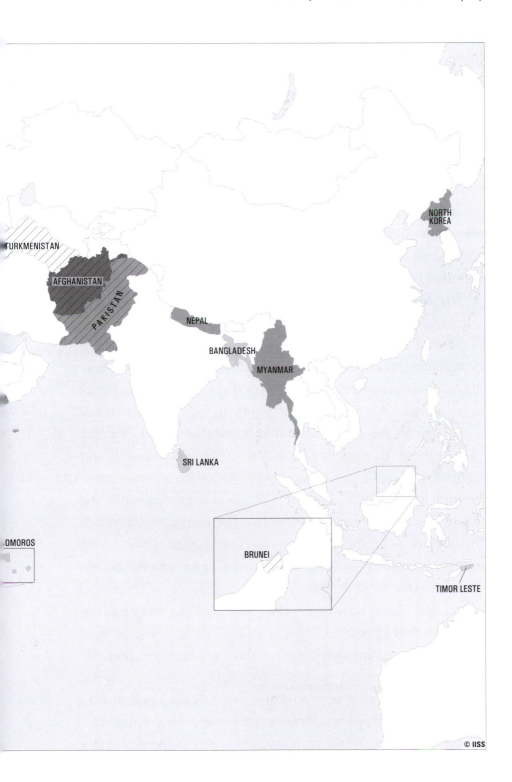

TURKMENISTAN

AFGHANISTAN

PAKISTAN

NEPAL

BANGLADESH

MYANMAR

SRI LANKA

NORTH KOREA

COMOROS

BRUNEI

TIMOR LESTE

© IISS

vulnerability, there is an imperfect correspondence between those states whose overall circumstances put them at greatest risk of failure and those most vulnerable to climate change. A recent attempt to identify national indicators of vulnerability and capacity to adapt to climate-related mortality, for example, distinguished between proxy measures reflecting immediate vulnerability and those reflecting the capacity to adapt over time. Adaptive capacity was 'associated predominantly with governance, civil and political rights, and literacy'.[49] The study was undertaken explicitly to provide indicators for vulnerability and adaptive capacity to climate change that were not captured by other indices.

The map on pages 106–7 compares the countries most vulnerable to climate change to the states identified as at particular risk of failure in the various empirical rankings. There is broad correspondence, with the ten countries for which there is greatest consensus on fragility – all of them are, with the exceptions of Iraq, Afghanistan and Haiti, in sub-Saharan Africa – also among the most vulnerable to climate change. But the consensus on fragility is just as strong for Côte d'Ivoire and Zimbabwe. The former is highly vulnerable to climate change (though it is not among the most vulnerable group), while the latter is only moderately so. Among the countries for which the consensus on fragility is not as strong, almost two-thirds are highly vulnerable to climate change, again mostly in sub-Saharan Africa, while most of the exceptions – Myanmar, Nepal and North Korea – lie elsewhere. Among the group of countries that appear among the 30 weakest states in at least one of the three rankings, only one-third are highly vulnerable to climate change and another third highly to moderately so. On the other hand, seven countries, the bulk yet again in sub-Saharan Africa, appear relatively stable yet highly vulnerable to climate change. While such assessments of vulnerability are preliminary and have weaknesses similar to attempts to assess state fragility quantitatively, the differences are nevertheless instructive.

Firstly, while sub-Saharan Africa emerges as the region of greatest concern for vulnerability to climate change, in keeping with the conventional wisdom, the weak correspondence between the most vulnerable and most fragile states (with the exception of the weakest, failing or already failed states) suggests that while climate change will be a threat multiplier in the aggregate, in specific cases the increased threat may be as much qualitative as quantitative. Secondly, outside sub-Saharan Africa, the correlation between the most fragile and most vulnerable states is even weaker, to the point of non-existence. Some relatively stable states such as Brunei and Qatar are highly vulnerable to climate change, while some weak states such as Bangladesh and Myanmar appear, contrary to conventional wisdom, more resilient. This may be due to the nature of the expected impacts; Bangladesh, for example, has always been vulnerable to extreme weather events, and has developed coping systems which pre-adapt it to climate change. Where climate impacts are unprecedented or unanticipated, states will be less able to cope even if they have the willingness and capacity.

Sub-Saharan Africa, and the Sahel region in particular, is where the greatest concentration both of fragile states and states vulnerable to climate change is found. Even though climate models show their poorest match with reality in the Sahel, and projections remain especially uncertain with regard to the timing and extent of the rainy season, there are increasing concerns over future stability given the particular history of fragility and conflict in the region.[50]

Although there is no apparent link between historical rainfall and conflict in the Sahel, a recent study has shown a correlation between civil war and temperature in sub-Saharan Africa after precipitation, per capita income and levels of democracy are taken into account. It projects an increase in armed conflict from an average of 11% of countries to 16.9% in a given year by 2030.[51] Since the change in average temperature over the continent is expected to be relatively uniform over this period, and the influence of precipitation appears to be negligible, there is little difference in the projected increase in violence between different parts of sub-Saharan Africa, including the Sahel. The results suggest that the temperature–conflict link is finely grained, however, so that year-on-year climate fluctuations will continue to be important, despite the clearly discernable increase in average temperature expected in the region over this period.[52]

Climate change over the next few decades will contribute to continued volatility, instability and conflict in the region, and perhaps to a quantitative increase in violence; but whether there will be a qualitative change sufficient to affect nations outside the region is another matter. That would entail not increased instability in already fragile states, but a step-change in relatively stable ones. Ghana and Burkina Faso are, for example, among the least fragile states in West Africa, although they both face considerable development challenges. Climate change could affect stability in Ghana by exacerbating internal tensions between south and north over water management; increasing instability in neighbouring states; and causing reductions in export crops such as cocoa. Burkina Faso faces many of the stresses that have caused problems elsewhere in the Sahel, including Sudan: water and food security, relations between farmers and herders, and migration. Such factors are only likely to be determining factors in instability and violence over the long term and in the more extreme scenarios.[53] Nevertheless, even if the likelihood that less severe climate change over the short to medium term could slow development and exacerbate existing problems in such countries to the point of crisis is lower than the likelihood that such change will push more fragile states over the brink, it poses a greater risk to international security. The comparative increased risk of instability is greater.

This two-pronged threat, of increased volatility for the most fragile states and increased risk for more stable ones, is present outside Africa too. In states of particular concern for international stability and for major Western powers, climate change could make things more difficult in the short and medium term. North Korea, for example, suffers periodic and chronic famine due to a combination of poor governance and environmental conditions such as drought and flooding, which will increase even with the relatively modest climate change projected for North Asia over the next few decades. Iran is also highly susceptible to increased drought over the next few decades, as well as more severe storms and floods.[54]

The repressive regime in Myanmar, which poses a lesser geopolitical threat, is already suffering from an increase in extreme weather events, such as 2008's Cyclone Nargis. The impacts of these events are made worse by the loss of coastal mangrove forests due to human activity.[55] Climate change will only worsen this trend: under natural conditions mangroves can adapt to the rate of expected warming and sea-level rise, but where the land into which they would normally expand is already subject to intensive human use this will be impossible.[56] In contrast, neighbouring Bangladesh has reduced its vulnerability to the effects of climate change through a policy of deliberate protection of coastal mangrove forests, bucking the global trend of deforestation. It has also adopted storm-alert systems and social support networks. Differences in governance, flexibility and resilience (all aspects of adaptive capacity) explain why deaths from natural disasters have risen in Myanmar but dropped in Bangladesh in recent years.[57]

In places with ongoing fighting against Islamist militants, climate change will add to the problems. Drought already contributes to instability in parts of Iraq, and any increase in frequency or severity will only make things worse.[58] The same dynamic exists in Afghanistan, with the added complication that climate change will affect opium production. Extreme winter weather recently damaged the poppy crop, but extended drought conditions in general favour poppy production over other crops.[59] Changes in seasonal precipitation volumes and intensity, and melting of Himalayan glaciers will also mean both increased flooding and water scarcity in Pakistan, hampering efforts to restore stability to parts of the country that offer havens to both local and foreign insurgents and international terrorist networks.[60] The impact of climate change over the next few decades may also reduce the chances of resolving Arab–Israeli tensions: issues of water, land and refugees are already central to the dispute; reduced economic growth could lead to greater poverty, social instability and extremism; and failure by the West to take effective climate-mitigation measures could reinforce political grievances.[61]

Some less fragile states

Less than a decade ago Indonesia and Colombia were both failing states.[62] Since then they have bounced back, mainly through economic growth and stability; they are both considered 'in danger' in the FSI and as belonging, by the Brookings criteria, to a second tier of fragile states (beyond those classified as weak) 'because they may still serve as significant breeding grounds for transnational security threats'.[63] Although they are not particularly vulnerable to climate change by the criteria used in the map on pages 106–7, Colombia and Indonesia are examples of the type of 'stronger' fragile state where the real differential impact of climate change will be felt.

Colombia: water security

When the current president of Colombia, Álvaro Uribe Vélez, was elected in 2002, the country faced high unemployment, two major left-wing insurgencies, widespread right-wing paramilitary activity, and extensive narcotics production and trafficking. Increased counter-insurgency efforts against the guerrillas and demobilisation of paramilitaries have improved the security situation, although the Revolutionary Armed Forces of Colombia (FARC) still maintains control of large portions of the country and reaps significant revenues from the drugs trade. Until the global financial crisis of 2008–2009, the economy was significantly improving, due to the better security environment, rising commodity prices and increased foreign investment. Levels of political violence and organised crime, poverty and unemployment, and internally displaced persons, however, remain high, while both the security and economic gains are precarious. FARC continues to launch attacks and demobilised paramilitaries have regrouped into armed gangs. GDP growth dropped significantly in 2008 and went into recession in 2009, and social unrest led Uribe to declare a state of emergency.[64]

Climate change may affect the ability of Colombia to maintain and improve on the progress it has achieved over the last decade. Precipitation and temperature changes in the high Andes are already being observed in the late twentieth century there was a warming of 0.2–0.3°C and a decrease in monthly rainfall of 2–3mm per decade. Projections suggest that the temperature increase could be 1–3°C by 2050, with an even greater rate of decline in rainfall.[65] Yields of most major food crops are projected to fall by around 5% by 2030. The Colombian economy is also highly vulnerable to climate-driven impacts on fisheries. So although the country is only moderately sensitive to climate-driven impacts on food production, it is highly exposed and its adaptive capacity is low.[66] The disease burden is expected to increase as temperature and rainfall changes create optimal conditions for mosquitoes, and expand their range, exposing a greater proportion of the population to malaria and dengue fever.[67]

The principal climate threat facing Colombia, however, involves water. In the tropical Andes, climate change, glaciers, water resources and a largely poor population 'meet in a critical nexus', with many shrinking glaciers destined to reach the point of no return within 10–20 years.[68] High-resolution climate simulations suggest that projected temperature increases and changes in precipitation could disrupt water and power supplies to large segments of the population.[69] At current rates of melting, there is a 90% probability that Colombia's glaciers will disappear by 2035. The *páramos*, a unique alpine grassland ecosystem that acts as a buffer to regulate glacier run-off, is expected to be reduced by over 50% by 2050 due to deforestation and over-grazing. Some 25% of Colombia's population depends on water from this resource.[70]

Colombia may already be feeling the impact of climate change on water security. A drought in 2009–2010 damaged coffee, cocoa and other crops, leading to high food prices and inflation; dropping river levels damaged fisheries; widespread forest fires led to a state of emergency being declared; and water rationing was imposed in major cities and municipalities throughout the country.[71] The drought was related to a cyclical ENSO event – El Niños in the late twentieth century also led to water rationing – but the latest crisis was particularly severe and the impact of such cyclical events is expected to continue to increase with rising mean temperatures.

The drought led to cutbacks in hydroelectric production, diversion of natural-gas supplies from transport to power generation, cutbacks in electricity exports to Venezuela and Ecuador, and the prospect of similar cutbacks in exports of natural gas. This posed a threat to Venezuela's economy, which was struggling with its own water and power rationing, and aggravated tensions that were already high following Colombia's decision in 2009 to allow the US military access to bases and facilities.[72] Venezuelan President Hugo Chávez, who had been using the confrontation with Colombia as a political distraction from his own domestic problems, declared that Colombia's actions were deliberately provocative.

Given Bogotá's status as a staunch US ally and, at least for now, a right-wing balancer to the general leftward trend in Latin American politics, and the role of Venezuela as an international spoiler, the geopolitical stakes are high. Climate change will make a reversal of Colombia's progress and a return to violence more likely. At the very least, it will make the country's remaining challenges, such as managing the global economic downturn, improving its poor human-rights record and resisting a tendency towards authoritarianism, harder to surmount.

Indonesia: food security

Indonesia was badly hit by the Asian financial crisis in 1997, which caused widespread social unrest and political instability, leading to the downfall of the Suharto regime that had ruled for three decades. Plagued by sectarian violence and centrifugal tendencies after Timor Leste achieved independence in 1999, it was viewed by many observers as at risk of state failure or even collapse and disintegration. Over the last decade many of these problems have been resolved, with free elections, an autonomy agreement ending the long-running separatist insurgency in Aceh province, and a robust counter-terrorism effort reducing the sectarian threat. A striking economic revival was threatened in May 2008 by rising food and fuel prices, which led to street protests, but the country has achieved a remarkable degree of stability, cohesion and increasing prosperity. Even in the face of the global financial crisis, Indonesia is expected to see continued modest economic growth.[73]

Indonesia's success story, like Colombia's, is potentially threatened by climate change. Over the longer term, the country is vulnerable to the full range of climate impacts, especially sea-level rise.[74] In the short to medium term, however, food insecurity will be the greatest risk. Annual mean temperature has increased in Indonesia by around 0.3°C from 1990 to 2005, and is expected to increase on average by another 0.36–0.47°C by 2020, with higher temperatures in the Moluccas and Borneo.[75] Rainfall projections are inconsistent and unreliable, but the rainy season is expected to be shorter, so regardless of whether rainfall increases or decreases, overall there will be an increased risk of flooding and drought.[76] As was the case for Colombia, the ENSO event in 1997 had a significant effect on food security, damaging over 400,000 hectares of rice as well as income-generating crops such as coffee, cocoa and rubber.[77] The impact of such events is expected to increase; it has been suggested that Indonesia's future climate will look very much like a permanent ENSO event.[78] By 2050, the chance that natural climate variability, including ENSO events, will have a significant effect on agricultural production in Java and Bali in any given year will increase markedly. These areas account for around 55% of the country's rice production.[79] The adaptations necessary to cope with these impacts include increased imports of rice stocks to buffer prices, improved water storage and irrigation infrastructure, adopting new, drought-tolerant rice varieties, crop diversification, improved access to ENSO forecasts, credit and insurance for farmers, and agricultural information and advice.[80] The country is highly sensitive to climate-driven impacts on fisheries up to 2050 and its adaptive capacity is low, but low exposure over this period means it is only moderately vulnerable.[81]

Indonesia is currently self-sufficient in food, but overall nutritional standards are poor and the country remains highly vulnerable to food insecurity. Chronic food insecurity in some areas stems not from unavailability but from barriers to access such as the aftermath of natural disasters, social instability, unemployment and high prices.[82] The impact of climate change on agriculture will increase the risk and widen the already substantial gap between rich and poor. This will probably not be enough to directly influence stability, and so long as the country remains relatively stable it should, with some outside support, be able to adapt to climate change over the medium term. But if other pressures lead to a reversal of Indonesia's progress, the added stress of climate change could accelerate the trend. This in turn would reinforce the structural barriers that already lead to localised food insecurity. The west and south of Sumatra and the west and east of Java are the areas most vulnerable to climate hazards. Parts of Java, particularly around Jakarta, are the most vulnerable regions in all of Southeast Asia – despite having high adaptive capacity – since they are exposed to most climate-related hazards and are so densely populated.[83] A differential impact of climate change within the country could lead to a revival of separatism.

Indonesia is, in a sense, the key to Southeast Asia: if it continues to evolve into a stable democracy with a robust emerging economy, it will enhance security throughout the region and the Asia-Pacific as a whole, and serve as a political model for the rest of the Muslim world. But if it reverts to instability or even collapse, it will be highly destabilising geopolitically.[84] Climate change could be a key factor in influencing its trajectory.

The bottom line

Indonesia's course over the last decade – defying most observers' predictions – illustrates the difficulty of forecasting the trajectory of weak or failing states, even without the added uncertainties surrounding climate trends and fluctuations. However, with the relative weight of climate change in influencing state stability set to increase over the next few decades, understanding its role can help refine such warnings and contribute to the formulation of appropriate responses. After all, predictions can fail to come true when they are treated as warnings and heeded.

CHAPTER FIVE

Climate Change and Security

When the UN's Framework Convention on Climate Change was adopted in 1994 with a mandate to 'prevent dangerous anthropogenic interference with the climate system ... within a time frame sufficient to allow ecosystems to adapt naturally to climate change, to ensure that food production is not threatened and to enable economic development to proceed in a sustainable manner', the term 'dangerous' was left undefined.[1] In its Third Assessment Report in 2001 the IPCC suggested that a global rise in temperature of 3°C over the next century would probably be manageable.[2] Since then, however, there has been considerable convergence of opinion among scientists, economists and policymakers that the global temperature increase should be contained to 2°C above pre-industrial levels – a 'guardrail' beyond which 'the possibilities for adaptation of society and ecosystems rapidly decline, with an increasing risk of social disruption through health impacts, water shortages and food insecurity'.[3] The choice of 2°C was based on the IPCC's synthesis of five 'reasons for concern' – risks to unique and threatened systems, risks from extreme climate events, distribution of impacts, aggregate impacts, and risks from future large-scale discontinuities – in the 2001 report. However, an update of this analysis using the same methodology and the most recent research suggests that the 2°C guardrail is insufficient to avoid dangerous impacts in the first two areas, and that the risk of large-scale discontinuities at the 2°C level is moderate rather than very low, as was previously reported.[4] It is still possible to have a reasonable chance of keeping warming below the guardrail, but even the drastic emissions reductions necessary to achieve this will have little effect on temperature increases over the next few decades. These will approach if not exceed a 1.5°C increase above pre-industrial levels, a target advocated by most of the world's most vulnerable countries in negotiations at the 2009 climate conference in Copenhagen.

The best estimates for global warming to the end of the century range from 2.5–4.7°C above pre-industrial levels, depending on the scenario. Even in the best-case scenario, the low end of the likely range is 1.8°C, and in the worst 'business as usual' projections, which actual emissions have been matching, the range of likely warming runs from 3.1–7.1°C. Even keeping emissions at constant 2000 levels (which have already been exceeded), global temperature would still be expected to reach 1.2°C (0.9–1.5°C) above pre-industrial levels by the end of the century.[5] Without early and severe reductions in emissions, the effects of climate change in the second half of the twenty-first century are likely to be catastrophic for the stability and security of countries in the developing world – not to mention the associated human tragedy.

Climate change could even undermine the strength and stability of emerging and advanced economies, beyond the knock-on effects on security of widespread state failure and collapse in developing countries.[6] And although they have been condemned as melodramatic and alarmist, many informed observers believe that unmitigated climate change beyond the end of the century could pose an existential threat to civilisa-tion.[7] What is certain is that there is no precedent in human experience for such rapid change or such climatic conditions, and even in the best case adaptation to these extremes would mean profound social, cultural and political changes.

Effective mitigation of climate change, to be sure, will also entail drastic change. To stabilise atmospheric concentrations of greenhouse gases, which are already at levels that will lead to warming of 2.0–2.4°C, global emissions would have to be reduced by 60–80% immediately. Such an immediate cut is not possible, but serious reductions must at least begin now if we are to have a reasonable chance of keeping within the 2°C guardrail. Otherwise, within ten years of business as usual (with emissions increasing by 2% annually) the rate of necessary reduction will exceed 5% a year.[8] Although the December 2009 UNFCCC conference in Copenhagen failed to achieve its goal of a legally binding agreement on global and national targets for emissions to keep warming below 2°C, the Copenhagen Accord drafted in negotiations between the United States and the BASIC countries – Brazil, South Africa, India and China – reiterated the guardrail and called for all nations to submit, for the first time, their own explicit emissions targets for 2020, for which progress would be measured, reported and veri-fied. Because of a few hold-outs (Bolivia, Cuba, Nicaragua, Sudan and Venezuela) the conference did not reach consensus on the accord, but rather 'took note' of it, legitimising in the UN process what was essentially an agreement among a small number of developed and emerging economies. The accord also included a commitment from developed countries to provide an additional $30 billion in 2010–2012, rising to $100bn per year from public and private sources by 2020 to assist developing countries in mitigation of emissions, preservation of forests, and adaptation to climate change.[9]

By the deadline of 31 January 2010, 55 countries, which collectively account for 78% of global emissions, had submitted their emissions-reductions targets to 2020 under the accord. The pledges did not reflect any new ambition beyond previously stated aspirations, and in some cases were weaker, hedged with caveats. These reductions, even if they are achieved, will thus fall well below what is necessary to avoid crossing the 2°C threshold.[10]

Most of the major industrial and industrialising nations, which are responsible for the vast majority of greenhouse-gas emissions, thus recognise the imperative to take concerted international action to reduce those emissions and mitigate the worst consequences of climate change. Although the overall costs, and the costs to individual national economies, will be high, the evidence indicates that the cost of inaction will in the long term be higher. There will be a trade-off between the costs of mitigation, and adaptation to the effects of climate change. And regardless of how successful attempts to reduce emissions may be, there will inevitably be some degree of warming, climate change and geopolitical consequences.

Paradox and policy

The IPCC's best-case and worst-case projections for global warming do not represent upper and lower limits on possible, or even likely, futures, but are rather 'best' and 'worst' within the context of the standard scenario sets devised to allow inter-comparison of various studies and to represent the likely range of unpredictable futures. They assume no policy-driven mitigation of emissions, so emissions reductions such as those to which various nations and groupings have already voluntarily committed (unilaterally or under the Copenhagen Accord and other agreements) can, as intended, reduce the projected warming. This much is trivial. The differences between the scenarios are significant, however, not just for emissions but for estimates of impact costs and the ability to adapt to climate change. Projected baseline global GDP growth by 2020 differs by more than a factor of two between scenarios. Greater wealth means more is at stake, but also means more adaptive capacity, at least for countries with the minimum levels of governance and legitimacy.

The scenarios also tend to assume, perhaps over-optimistically, that the gap between rich and poor nations will narrow, so that the ratio of per capita incomes between developed and developing countries will go from 16:1 in 1990 to 6–8:1 in 2020 and 1.5–3:1 by 2100. They also make assumptions about the rate and direction of technological change and global governance.[11] But the projection of these trends into the future ignores the fact that the impacts of climate change will affect all these factors – global wealth disparity, technology and governance – negatively, so that the more severe the early impacts are the less likely it will be that the world continues down a particular path. The scenarios also assume no policy-driven adaptation measures. Impact studies compare climate-change scenarios to a putative future under the same development assumptions rather than to the present, so that the numbers of people experiencing water or food insecurity, or exposed to extreme weather events, for example, may be lower than at present – but higher than they would have been without climate change.

In some studies, moreover, it is simply assumed that countries with per capita GDP above a certain level, say \$6,000 – a level which Colombia, for example, may have exceeded for the first time in 2009 – have the adaptive capacity to cope with particular impacts, and these countries are excluded from the analysis.[12] But there can also be spontaneous adaptations, such as migration, changes in population, changes in crop patterns, etc. that do not involve top-down implementation. There is a two-pronged uncertainty principle at work, whereby feedbacks alter both essentially arbitrary assumptions about future trends and policy-driven action in unpredictable ways.[13]

Mitigation of climate change, through reducing emissions of greenhouse gases, shifting to carbon-neutral energy sources such as biofuels, or reducing CO_2 concentrations through reforestation, is the only way of avoiding the most dire consequences of global warming, which would exceed the capacity of individuals, nations or the international system to adapt. Mitigation and adaptation are for the most part complementary responses to global warming (although sometimes, as in the case of conversion of agricultural or forest land to biofuel production, mitigation efforts can make the impacts worse). Some warming is inevitable, and the ability to adapt spontaneously or through policy-driven processes is the critical variable across all spatial and temporal scales, not just for avoiding social collapse or state failure.

Below a critical temperature threshold, the rate at which the climate changes and the amount of increased variability can be more important than the absolute amount of average warming, since adaptation can never be instantaneous. There is a learning curve for individuals and institutions, and investments in infrastructure take time. Large agricultural investments – changing crops, for example – can take 15–30 years to come to fruition.[14] Empirical analysis of the relationship between climate and economic growth over the last half-century has shown that, on aggregate, adaptation takes at least ten years to have an effect.[15] If the rate of climate change accelerates, as is likely, this will become even more critical. Improving adaptive capacity through state-building, democratisation, strengthening civil society and so on can be a lengthy process too, and one less certain of success. Spontaneous adaptation, moreover, is not controllable and can lead to major unexpected upheavals, such as large-scale migration.

Adaptation is not just a question of being able to cope with new climate conditions, but also with new socio-economic conditions created by efforts to mitigate climate change. One of the biggest political stumbling blocks to effective climate-change mitigation in the United States, for example, is the reluctance of legislators from coal-producing states to support efforts that will of necessity lead to reduced coal consumption.[16] Similarly, oil-producing states negotiated for a buffer against the economic impact of a premature shift away from oil. For the first time, the impact of 'response measures' was included as a criterion for eligibility for adaptation funding under the Copenhagen Accord.

Climate change thus presents policymakers in the developed world with two different questions: one of response and one of prevention. Where will new or increased military or humanitarian interventions likely be needed due to acute crises caused by climate change? And how best to prioritise adaptation funds and other forms of aid or support to avoid chronic problems caused or exacerbated by climate change?

Strategic implications

The inherent uncertainty of climate projections is of a part with a more general problem of uncertainty in strategic planning, and defence planning in particular. On the one hand, the future is impossible to predict; on the other, without some guidance as to what is likely to happen planning becomes impossible too. There is always a temptation to rely on quantitative models for such guidance, on the principle that, although undoubtedly inaccurate in detail, they are better than nothing. But this may not be the case, if they draw attention to the wrong places. Rather than focus on particular cases, planners need to expect the unexpected, and focus on an increasing range of variability rather than simply the direction of the underlying trend. Militaries are particularly good at planning for such wide variability; although it is easy to point to specific failures for organisational or personality-related reasons, successes are often invisible.[17]

With regard to climate, the three main sources of uncertainty – models, scenarios and annual variability – are important over different timescales. Over the short term, and particularly for regional or smaller-scale projections, choice of scenario matters little and variability predominates, while over the longer term scenario and model become critical. Although the long-term warming trend is already distinguishable against annual variability globally and in most regions of the world, precipitation trends, which depend critically on models, are not. In many areas, particularly Latin America and Africa, even the direction of the trend by the end of the century cannot be projected with confidence. In East Africa, an increase in precipitation is only expected to be discernable within 60 years of the baseline period – that is, by 2045–2065 – and in Central America within 65 years. In Asia (with the exception of Central Asia) an increase is expected to be noticeable within 15–28 years.[18] Over the next few decades, however, the quality and sophistication of regional and medium-term forecasts should continue to improve, so there must be a continual adjustment in the balance between flexibility and prediction.

When it comes to state instability and the aggregate threat it poses to international order, climate change is indeed a threat multiplier. But it is not necessarily any more so than any of the other causes or contributors to instability – no single factor is either necessary or sufficient. What makes current climate change unique is that it is a new variable; other causal factors – including natural climate variation – have always been with us, but human-induced warming is directional, accelerating and (on the timescales that matter) irreversible.

The multi-causal nature of the climate–security nexus works both ways: while climate change may act as a threat multiplier in conjunction with political, economic or social factors, such factors can reduce the ability of a society to implement measures to mitigate the effects of environmental impacts of climate change, thus acting as threat multipliers for environmental stresses. There is a system of mutual feedback, with climate-induced environmental stress affecting state and social cohesion as well as direct human security, and a weakness in state and social institutions contributing to more severe environmental impacts.

There will undoubtedly be climate-related conflicts over the next several decades, as there have been in the past. Given the time frame there may be fewer than the conventional wisdom would have it, but it is necessary to be prepared to respond directly through military or humanitarian interventions and to cope with social and political consequences. It should be noted that the greater the suppression of long-term change by medium-term cyclic factors, the more abrupt the impacts will be at mid-century. Medium-term cooling or slowing of climate change does not mean that the longer-term trend is any less; in fact, in a few decades' time, when those cycles that run counter to the longer-term trend begin rather to reinforce it, the rate of change will accelerate, creating a sudden shock to the system.

The problem of climate-induced instability goes beyond a simple quantitative increase in the humanitarian and security consequences of state failure, internal conflict or collapse, such as increased ethnic rivalries, creation of safe havens or recruiting grounds for terrorists and the costs of intervention. Militaries are often the only institutions with the capacity to deploy rapidly in response to humanitarian crises caused by natural disasters, and armed forces will face increased demands as such crises multiply and intensify with the increase in frequency and severity of extreme weather events, aggravated by sea-level rise. The US military deployed troops externally to Honduras after Hurricane Mitch in 1998 and to Haiti after Hurricane Jeanne in 2004, and internally to Mississippi and Louisiana after Katrina in 2005. The international responses to the 2004 Indian Ocean tsunami, the 2005 Kashmir earthquake, Cyclone Nargis in Myanmar in 2008, and the earthquake in Haiti in January 2010 all involved military resources and personnel from many developed and developing countries. While some of these disasters are not climate related, this sort of disaster response is likely to be increasingly needed as the climate changes. Since the 2008 earthquake in Sichuan, for example, China has begun to place special emphasis on capabilities for domestic and international disaster and humanitarian relief.[19] Although Taiwan is cutting back on defence spending due to the need to divert funds to recovery from disasters such as Typhoon Morakot in 2009, at the same time it is aiming to improve the military's disaster-relief capabilities.[20]

If militaries from developed countries find themselves less able to cope than at present with such crises through overstretch, cutbacks or both, there will not only be a global increase in humanitarian problems, but a loss of prestige and soft power and even a negative reaction to a perceived uncaring West. A widening gap between rich and poor on a global scale, and within individual countries, may create a revolution of frustrated expectations as countries and individuals perceive that they are not receiving their fair share of the global commons. This will be exacerbated by an increased north–south divide, especially over the medium term, as the physical effects of climate change tend to affect developing regions more – for the same broad environmental and geophysical reasons that influenced the development of the advanced economies in the first place. At the African Union summit in January 2007, Ugandan President Yoweri Museveni called global warming 'an act of aggression by the rich against the poor'.[21] Al-Qaeda has frequently blamed America for global warming in propaganda videos and audiotapes.[22] Reluctance to acknowledge equity issues with regard to the principle of 'common but differentiated responsibility' to reduce greenhouse-gas emissions, a main stumbling block in the failure of Washington to ratify the Kyoto Protocol and a continuing barrier to efforts to pass effective climate-change mitigation legislation in the United States, will only exacerbate this tendency.

Perhaps the most important security impact of climate change, as both a cause and consequence of state instability and failure, will be an increase in cross-border migration and internal population displacement. Viewed from the perspective of the individuals involved, migration can be an effective or necessary adaptation strategy to climate change, but its impact on the stability of already fragile states can be severe, and resulting conflict can be a driver of further migration, as the pre-modern record of cultural response to climate change demonstrates. This was the precise dynamic at work in Darfur. Estimates of the number of environmentally induced migrants range as high as 200 million by 2050, although the numbers are extremely difficult to estimate and strongly depend on assumptions about overall population growth.[23] To put this in perspective, at the end of 2008, there were some 42m forcibly displaced persons worldwide, four-fifths of them in developing countries.[24]

The 2010 US Quadrennial Defense Review reflected all these concerns. It concluded that:

> Climate change could have significant geopolitical impacts around the world, contributing to poverty, environmental degradation, and the further weakening

of fragile governments. Climate change will contribute to food and water scarcity, will increase the spread of disease, and may spur or exacerbate mass migration. While climate change alone does not cause conflict, it may act as an accelerant of instability or conflict, placing a burden to respond on civilian institutions and militaries around the world. In addition, extreme weather events may lead to increased demands for defence support to civil authorities for humanitarian assistance or disaster response.[25]

Making the right future

Hopes that a new international climate-mitigation regime might lead to new institutions (perhaps a World Environmental Organisation on the model of the World Trade Organisation) and new powers or roles for existing institutions that would help structure international relations in the next century as much as the Bretton Woods Agreement and its offshoots did for the post-war era, were dashed by the failure of the Copenhagen conference to achieve a binding global agreement. One person's hopes are another's fears; the main roadblock at Copenhagen was the reluctance, or rather refusal, of major emerging economies such as China and India to accept the formal restraints on their sovereignty that the necessary reporting and enforcement mechanisms would require, and there is by no means consensus among elites or popular opinion in the developed world either that any such restraints are desirable or necessary. The issue is highly polarising, and regardless of the merits, whatever the outcome of further negotiations within or outside the UNFCCC process, it is unlikely that an overarching regime will be established.

Despite its importance in the long term, mitigation of climate change will incur both political and economic costs in the short term in return for nebulous and imprecise benefits further down the line. There is greater unrealised potential for international cooperation to cope with and adapt to the impacts of climate change, especially on the regional or bilateral level, than there is for mitigation efforts. Regional agreements on water-resource management have been both effective in their own right and have had a wider stabilising effect even in potential trouble spots such as the Jordan River Valley and between India and Pakistan. The opportunity exists for strengthening regional institutions and security in Latin America, Africa and Southeast Asia, in particular, in response to increasing water scarcity. The greatest potential for enhancing international security in the face of climate change, however, lies in assisting in national-level adaptation to reduce the chance of state failure, instability and conflict.

In Darfur, for example, an understanding of the contribution of climate change to the conflict can help in formulating policies to promote development and prevent future violence. If the goal is to determine guilt and achieve justice for past violence (as in the move by the International Criminal Court in March 2009 to indict Sudanese President Omar al-Bashir for genocide, war crimes and crimes against humanity over the fighting in Darfur), or to resolve an ongoing conflict, the contribution of environmental degradation caused by climate change is perhaps not relevant. In the case of Darfur, moreover, as in many other cases around the world, the goals of justice and conflict resolution or prevention are not always congruent. The indictment of Bashir has been a major factor in perpetuating the fighting in Darfur and blocking attempts by the international community to ameliorate the consequences. However, if the goal is to prevent future conflict and instability, for reasons of humanitarianism, realpolitik or both, understanding environmental causality is critical to determining appropriate adaptation measures. Successful strategies emphasise participatory, community development that empowers at the local level, creates more diversity in livelihoods, manages natural resources and hedges against income and resource variability.[26] To be effective in a weak or failed state, such adaptation efforts require a previous restoration and strengthening of good governance and civil society.

On the broadest level, there is no real contradiction between humanitarian and security goals. The main consequences of state failure or economic and social collapse involve human insecurity, which in turn leads to conflict and other security threats. Conflict prevention or preventing state failure for selfish, hard security reasons thus also enhances human security. The need for a capability for immediate action, especially with regard to disaster relief, will continue and even increase as the climate changes. But when it comes to the incremental contribution of climate change to insecurity, the trade-off between ameliorating immediate humanitarian crises and supporting long-term development is less of an issue than the trade-off between direct sectoral adaptation priorities and general improvements in resilience.

Economic development, improving governance and democracy, and reducing corruption are all desirable on their own merits. Considered as adaptations to climate change such measures may be more important than mitigation, especially in the short to medium term, as mitigation efforts will take much longer to bear fruit. Building institutional capacity to increase adaptive capability will have the added benefit of improving the efficiency of mitigation efforts. Adaptation funding and programmes should not be conceived of in isolation, but as parts of an overall development approach to fragile states.[27] However, climate change may alter the balance of priorities within such an approach. The focus of adaptation efforts should not be on the worst cases – already failed or failing states – but rather on those fragile or recovering states which have proved able to cope but are at particular risk from climate change, and on states where failure would be most catastrophic for their neighbours and the rest of the world. This change in priorities must not be used, however, as a cynical excuse to count resources already being committed to general development towards national commitments to adaptation assistance.

It is impossible to put a precise figure on the cost of sectoral adaptation measures, since the impacts are imprecise. The UNFCCC put the annual global cost at \$40–170bn to 2030, of which \$27–66bn would be in developing countries, but the true figure could be two to three times as much.[28] Estimates of the cost for developing countries between 2010 and 2015 alone range from \$6–55bn to \$129–163bn.[29] International assistance towards such costs has so far been negligible. This is in part because much of the spending has been on preliminary planning and pilot programmes, and because it has taken time to set up the necessary multilateral institutional mechanisms to administer and disburse funds. For example, the Adaptation Fund set up under the 2001 Kyoto Protocol and controlled by developing countries, funded by a 2% levy on carbon credits issued by the Clean Development Mechanism, was not actually established until 2007 and as of the end of 2009 was yet to make any disbursements from its \$33.7m available.[30]

At the beginning of 2010, not counting the commitments in the Copenhagen Accord, some \$18.7bn had been pledged for a range of multilateral and bilateral funds to combat climate change. Much of this money, however, was earmarked for mitigation efforts or specifically for deforestation prevention and reforestation projects. Only \$2bn had actually been deposited, and only about a third of that had been dispersed. The principal conduits for adaptation efforts, besides the

UNFCCC Adaptation Fund, are the Japanese government's Cool Earth Partnership, of which 20% of the $10bn pledged is for adaptation; and the Least Developed Countries Fund and Special Climate Change Fund administered by the Global Environmental Facility, a partnership of 179 member governments and ten international organisations, including various UN programmes and international development banks. Total adaptation funds pledged to date, excluding commitments made under the Copenhagen Accord, are only a small percentage of the most optimistic estimates of the resources required.[31]

The $10bn a year from the developed countries over the next three years and the $100bn a year by 2020 called for in the Copenhagen Accord is intended as

> new and additional resources, including forestry and investments through international institutions ... with balanced allocation between adaptation and mitigation. Funding for adaptation will be prioritised for the most vulnerable developing countries, such as the least developed countries, small island developing States and Africa ... This funding will come from a wide variety of sources, public and private, bilateral and multilateral, including alternative sources of finance. New multilateral funding for adaptation will be delivered through effective and efficient fund arrangements, with a governance structure providing for equal representation of developed and developing countries. A significant portion of such funding should flow through the Copenhagen Green Climate Fund.[32]

It is unclear exactly where the money will come from, and despite pledges that this will be 'new' money, when the

Copenhagen Accord was agreed there had been no pledges towards the Global Environmental Facility's fifth replenishment cycle for all its programmes (not just climate change) for the middle of 2010.[33] It took nearly ten years to set up the Adaptation Fund, so the prognosis for the efficient and timely allocation of resources through the new Copenhagen Green Fund is not good. Even if it were, given the estimates of total adaptation costs, the total amount pledged would probably be insufficient even if it were all allocated to adaptation. This is unlikely on the track record; nor would it be desirable, since even the most effective practical adaptation possible in the developing world will become irrelevant in the second half of the century if mitigation efforts are unsuccessful.

Existing adaptation funding mechanisms under the UNFCCC, as well as the proposed Copenhagen Green Climate Fund, are subject to inefficiencies, compromises and political constraints that limit their effectiveness in enhancing human security and their utility to target funding with security considerations in mind. Other mechanisms are better in this respect, with the World Bank, for example, calling for a synthesis of security, governance and economics to be most effective in securing development.[34] Despite the inadequacy of current funding pledges compared to projected costs of adaptation, any additional funding from developed nations would be best targeted through such mechanisms or on a bilateral basis specifically to improve governance and resilience in response to specific national-security concerns, as part of a joined-up strategy. It will be expensive, but in the long run not as expensive as doing nothing. Similarly, the major industrial powers should include climate security in setting priorities for existing programmes.

Such an emphasis on national-security concerns need not be a promotion of selfish national interest at the expense of developing nations. The Brookings report on state weakness in the developing world, for example, which does not consider climate change, calls for increasing the priority of poverty alleviation in US policy; increasing assistance to the world's weakest states (especially in sub-Saharan Africa) and targeted to unique performance gaps in those countries; focusing on increasing security in failed and critically weak states; paying attention to severe performance gaps even in better-performing states; and coordination with other institutional actors, including the states of concern themselves.[35] There is nothing here that contradicts the recommendations for addressing fragile states in the context of climate change given above. The importance of climate change over the medium term is, in this respect at least, not so much as a threat multiplier but as a threat modifier, changing the relative balance of priorities.

CHAPTER SIX

Conclusion

This book set out to address a simple question: what are the implications of climate change over the next few decades for global security and international relations? It is clear that unmitigated climate change will be nothing less than disastrous for the global community. Without sharp and early reductions in emissions of greenhouse gases, the world will face profound disruption, human tragedy, and unforeseeable political, social and cultural consequences beginning in the second half of the twenty-first century, posing a threat to the liberal order. Over the longer term, it could even pose an existential threat to industrial civilisation. Although the precise trajectory of the future cannot be predicted with any certainty, contemplating such human and security consequences over the longer term provides stark justification for effective mitigation policies, and the sooner the better.

Other geopolitical consequences are likely over the short and medium term, from the next ten years to the middle of the century. Some, such as the opening of a new arena of international competition as the melting of the Arctic ice cap provides access to new resources and trade routes, are imminent.

Others, such as changes to international maritime boundaries due to rising sea levels, are longer-term challenges. Neither is examined in this book. Nor are the frightening consequences of so-called 'wild card' scenarios of abrupt climate change, despite estimates that the chance of such events is as high as 1–2%, a degree of risk that then US Vice President Dick Cheney argued should be treated as a certainty in terms of choosing the appropriate response to a national security threat, such as acquisition of a nuclear weapon by terrorists.[1] Abrupt climate change has the same low probability, but a higher impact. For strategic planning purposes, however, it is best to focus on the most likely rather than the most extreme cases. In this respect the main threat posed by climate change in the short to medium term – on the order of two to four decades – is state failure and internal conflict.

Evidence from what is known about the development of human civilisation in general, and in specific prehistoric to early modern societies across a range of complexity, reveals a close interaction between climate and political, social and cultural development. Periods of rapid global climate change during the last 10,000 years had varying regional consequences, and socio-cultural responses to global and regional climate change ranged from expansion to reorganisation to collapse. The ability to adapt depended on both physical capacities and pre-adaptive cultural traits. The historical precedents of climate-induced collapse tend to involve global or regional cooling rather than warming, but the post-industrial warming the world has already experienced is historically unprecedented. Projected global warming, even over the medium term, leads further into uncharted territory. Theoretical considerations indicate that the socio-political effects induced by such warming over the medium term will be similar to that experienced by past societies facing climate change. The relevance of early societies' responses to climate change might be limited because of qualitative differences between pre-industrial and industrial civilisation, and between a pre-globalised and globalised world. But though increased complexity may be a temporary buffer, it ultimately increases vulnerability.

Regional variation in historical climate change has always created winners and losers. With projected anthropogenic warming over the short and medium term, this may still be the case, although global interconnections now mean that the wider consequences of the impacts on the losers may outweigh any benefit to the luckier nations. In the longer term, there will be no real winners.

The key to disaggregating the contribution of climate change among other factors to state instability, conflict and security, particularly in terms of migration, conflict over resources and so on, is not whether climate change is either a necessary or sufficient cause, or even the most important empirical factor. Rather, it is whether, all other things being equal, climate change makes such developments more likely. The conflict in Darfur exemplifies the complexity of determining causation and the importance of context – of asking the right question – in making causal attributions. Just as no specific weather event can be definitively attributed to climate change because of normal variation within a complex system, specific social or political developments cannot be definitively attributed to climate or other environmental factors. But by the same logic, within a system of complex causality, such developments cannot be definitively attributed to any specific social, economic, political or contingent cause.

The whole question of the impact of climate change on conflict and security is fraught with uncertainty. Besides the opacity of complex causation, the normal uncertainties involved in strategic planning, especially beyond a time horizon of 20 or 30 years, are multiplied by the uncertainties involved in making long-term climate projections, including assumptions of population growth and development paths in the standardised scenarios and the feedbacks between those assumptions and the impacts of the climate change they create. 'Known unknowns' such as year-to-year variability in weather and climate (which is only expected to increase in response to global warming) are enough to make specific predictions meaningless, even beyond the inherent uncertainties of the scenarios and models. Given the global temperature trend and a projected increase in extremes of temperature and precipitation, however, an overall increase in instability is to be expected, even if it cannot be pinned down to specific times and places.

Over the long term, changes in water and food availability will be major drivers of insecurity, but in the medium term the trends will be as much a matter of incremental, quantitative change as of qualitative step change. Increased variability, especially increased frequency and severity of extreme events, will be the most significant factor, so relative vulnerability to such shocks will be the most significant national trait. Countries already living on the edge may be pushed into failure or collapse by such shocks, but if they are already that fragile, the increased security threat may be minimal from a global perspective. More important in that regard will be less fragile and regionally important states which could be nudged off the path of development and descend or retreat towards instability and failure.

Analysis of both pre-modern social and cultural responses to climate change and concepts of state failure indicates that adaptive capacity is the crucial variable in determining vulnerability to climate change. Successful adaptation across a range of sectors to avoid the potentially destabilising impacts of climate change in weak or failing states requires a minimum level of governance, accountability, civil society, public health and education. For the most fragile states, those on the cusp of failure or collapse, this must be the priority. For stronger states that already meet this minimum standard, adaptation efforts should be directed at specific vulnerabilities that pose the greatest risk to stability. Adaptation measures cannot be planned or implemented in isolation but must be part of an overall development approach to fragile states. Where developed nations target new adaptation assistance and existing development programmes in response to national-security concerns, this too cannot be done in isolation but must take into account multilateral efforts. Climate change must also be part of an overall approach to national security and defence planning.

The adaptive capacity of the developed countries and the more advanced emerging economies such as China, India, Brazil and South Africa will be more than sufficient to cope with medium-term climate change. But all such states, even the most advanced, will sooner or later reach a threshold beyond which they will face their own crises. The closer they get to this threshold, the less they will be willing or able to help ameliorate the impacts of climate change in less fortunate countries. It is therefore in the interest of all nations to keep climate change below the two-degree guardrail; although for many rising powers and most developing countries even this may not be sufficient. The rising powers do, however, view climate change as an issue of historical equity as much as geopolitics, and the developed nations must be prepared to compromise and provide support for the aspirations of the rising powers, lest they cut off the nose to spite the face.

The security dimension of climate change will come increasingly to the fore as countries face falls in available resources, economic vitality, increased stress on military capabilities, greater instability in regions of strategic import, and a widening gap between rich and poor. Over the next few decades, unavoidable global warming will lead to a world where a changing climate multiplies and intensifies current security concerns and creates new ones. Food, water and energy security are central to national and international security, and climate change will magnify them all. Instability, conflict and humanitarian disasters, both chronic and acute, are not the inevitable result of climate change, nor are they dependent on it. But over the course of history, climate change has affected the stability of societies, nations and civilisations and the unprecedented change that has already begun raises the spectre of increasing and accelerating social, geopolitical and economic disruption. Climate change will have to be taken into account in policy debates on issues involving anything but the shortest timescales.

GLOSSARY

4AR	Fourth Assessment Report
ACD	IISS Armed Conflict Database
BAU	Business as usual
BCE	Before the Common Era
CAR	Central African Republic
CE	Common Era
CIFP	Country Indicators for Foreign Policy
CNAS	Center for a New American Security
CSIS	Center for Strategic and International Studies
DRC	The Democratic Republic of the Congo
ENSO	El Niño–Southern Oscillation
FARC	Revolutionary Armed Forces of Colombia
FSI	Failed States Index
IDP	Internally displaced person
IISS	International Institute for Strategic Studies
IPCC	Intergovernmental Panel on Climate Change
ISW	Index of State Weakness in the Developing World
NIE	National Intelligence Estimate
PRIO	Peace Research Institute Oslo
SPLA/M	Sudan People's Liberation Army/Movement
SRES	IPCC Special Report on Emissions Scenaros

TAR	Third Assessment Report
UNEP	United Nations Environment Programme
UNFCCC	United Nations Framework Convention on Climate Change
WBGU	German Advisory Council on Global Change
WG1	IPCC Working Group 1
WG2	IPCC Working Group 2
WMO	World Meteorological Organisation

Introduction

1   For a comprehensive survey, assess-
    ment and synthesis of the sci-
    entific evidence up to 2006, see
    Intergovernmental Panel on Climate
    Change, *Climate Change 2007: The
    Physical Science Basis*, Working
    Group I Contribution to the Fourth
    Assessment Report (Cambridge:
    Cambridge University Press, 2007),
    hereinafter referred to as 4AR WG1.
    The Summary for Policymakers and
    Technical Summary are referred to as
    SPM and TS, respectively. For more
    recent evidence and its relationship to
    the consensus embodied in the Fourth
    Assessment Report see Chapter 1 of
    this book.

2   Paul F. Herman and Gregory F.
    Treverton, 'The Political Consequences
    of Climate Change', *Survival*, vol. 51,
    no. 2, April–May 2009, pp. 137–48. For
    the idea of climate change as a threat
    multiplier see also CNA Corporation,
    *National Security and the Threat of
    Climate Change* (Alexandria, VA:
    The CNA Corporation, 2007), http://
    securityandclimate.cna.org/report/
    National Security and the Threat of
    Climate Change.pdf.

3   See Naomi Oreskes, Testimony before
    the Committee on Environment
    and Public Works, United States
    Senate, 6 December 2006, available
    at http://www.stanford.edu/dept/
    cisst/ORESKES.Senate EPW.FINAL.
    pdf; Oreskes, 'The Long Consensus
    on Climate Change', *Washington
    Post*, 1 February 2007; Oreskes and
    Jonathan Renouf, 'Jason and the Secret
    Climate Change War', *Sunday Times*, 7
    September 2008. For more developed
    analyses and policy advocacy see
    Neville Brown, 'Climate and Conflict',
    RUSI Journal, vol. 135, Winter 1990,
    pp. 79–83; Brown, 'Climate, Ecology
    and International Security', *Survival*,
    vol. 31, November–December 1989,
    pp. 519–32; Ian B. Cowan, 'Security
    Implications of Global Climate
    Changes', *Canadian Defense Quarterly*,
    vol. 19, Autumn 1989, pp. 43–9; Patrice
    E. Greene, *Military Implications of Global
    Warming* (Carlisle Barracks, PA: Army
    War College, 1999), http://handle.
    dtic.mil/100.2/ADA363890; Thomas
    Homer-Dixon, *Environment, Scarcity
    and Violence* (Princeton, NJ: Princeton
    University Press, 1999).

4   See Oreskes, 'The Scientific Consensus on Climate Change: How Do We Know We're Not Wrong?', in Joseph F.C. DiMento and Pamela M. Doughman (eds), *Climate Change What It Means for Us, Our Children, and Our Grandchildren* (Cambridge, MA: MIT Press, 2007), pp. 65–99.

5   Al Gore, *An Inconvenient Truth: The Plantetary Emergency of Global Warming and What We Can Do About It* (Emmaus, PA: Rodale Books, 2006); Nicholas Stern, *The Economics of Climate Change: The Stern Review* (Cambridge: Cambridge University Press, 2006).

6   CNA Corporation, *National Security and the Threat of Climate Change*; Joshua W. Busby, *Climate Change and National Security: An Agenda for Action*, Council Special Report no. 32 (New York: Council on Foreign Relations, 2007); Kurt M. Campbell et al., *The Age of Consequences: The Foreign Policy and National Security Implications of Global Climate Change* (Washington DC: Center for Strategic and International Studies and Center for a New American Security, 2007); 'Climate Change: Security Implications and Regional Impacts', *Strategic Survey 2007* (Abingdon: Routledge for the IISS, 2007), pp. 46–69.

7   Ben Russell and Nigel Morris, 'Armed Forces are Put on Standby to Tackle Threat of Wars over Water', *Independent*, 28 February 2006; Secretary-General's Address to UNIS–UN Conference on Climate Change, New York, 1 March 2007, http://un.org/apps/sg/sgstats.asp?nid=2462; 'France Warns Climate Change Driving War, Hunger', AFP, 18 April 2008; 'Global Warming Threatens Asia-Pacific Security, Warns Australian PM', *Guardian*, 10 September 2008; 'Expert: Climate Change Could Mean "Extended World War"', AP, 23 February 2009.

8   Council of the European Union, *Climate Change and International Security*, Report from the Commission and the Secretary-General/High Representative to the European Council, 7249/08, Brussels, 3 March 2008; Andrew Clark, 'Climate Change Threatens Security, UK Tells UN', *Guardian*, 18 April 2007; Margaret Beckett, 'Climate Change: "The Gathering Storm"', Annual Winston Churchill Memorial Lecture, British American Business Inc., New York, 16 April 2007, available at http://collections.europarchive.org/tna/; Beckett, 'Opening Remarks', UN Security Council Debate on Energy, Climate and Security', New York, 17 April 2007, available at http://collections.europarchive.org/tna/.

9   R. Schubert et al., *Climate Change as a Security Risk* (London: Earthscan for the German Advisory Council on Global Change, 2008), p. 180.

Chapter One

1   4AR WG1 SPM. The IPCC assessment reports offer the most comprehensive summaries of the scientific evidence; for a good general discussion of the science aimed at policymakers and analysts see Richard Wolfson and Stephen H. Schneider, 'Understanding Climate Science', in S.H. Schneider et al. (eds), *Climate Change Policy: A Survey* (Washington DC: Island Press, 2002), pp. 3–51.

2   W.F. Ruddiman, *Plows, Plagues and Petroleum: How Humans Took Control of Climate* (Princeton, NJ: Princeton University Press, 2006); Tim Flannery, *The Weather Makers: Our Changing Climate and What it Means for Life on Earth* (London: Penguin, 2006), pp. 61–8; S. Vavrus et al., 'Climate Model Tests of the Anthropogenic Influence on Greenhouse-induced Climate Change: The Role of Early Human Agriculture, Industrialisation, and Vegetation Feedbacks', *Quarternary Science Reviews*, vol. 27, nos 13–14, July 2008, pp. 1,410–25. The cyclical nature of climate on a multi-millennial scale is discussed later in this chapter; the lesser but in human terms still significant variations since the end of the Ice Age are discussed in Chapter 2.

3   4AR WG1, p. 435. The IPCC uses the concept of 'radiative forcing', or the change in net irradiance at the top of the troposphere (the lowest level of the atmosphere, up to 9–16km above the surface). It is related linearly to global mean surface-temperature change (4AR WG1, pp. 133–4).

4   For the original hockey-stick graph, see Michael E. Mann et al., 'Global-scale Temperature Patterns and Climate Forcing over the Past Six Centuries', *Nature*, vol. 392, no. 6,678, 23 April 1998, pp. 779–87; Mann et al., 'Northern Hemisphere Temperatures during the Past Millennium: Inferences, Uncertainties, and Limitations', *Geophysical Research Letters*, vol. 26, no. 6, 15 March 1999, pp. 759–62; for summations of more recent work see 4AR WG1, p. 467; Mann et al., 'Proxy-based Reconstructions of Hemispheric and Global Surface Temperature Variations over the Past Two Millennia', *Proceedings of the National Academy of Sciences*, vol. 105, no. 36, 9 September 2008, pp. 13,252–7.

5   There was, to be sure, a high degree of climate instability before 10,000 years ago – the end of the last Ice Age – which had profound effects on human biological and cultural evolution. See William J. Burroughs, *Climate Change in Prehistory: The End of the Reign of Chaos* (Cambridge: Cambridge University Press, 2005).

6   For a detailed discussion of the definition of climate and its relevance for planners and policymakers see Nathaniel B. Guttman, 'Statistical Descriptors of Climate', *Bulletin of the American Meteorological Society*, vol. 70, no. 6, June 1989, pp. 602–7.

7   See Oreskes, 'The Scientific Consensus on Climate Change: How Do We Know We're Not Wrong?', p. 78.

8   Oreskes, 'The Scientific Consensus on Climate Change', *Science*, vol. 306, 3 December 2004, p. 1686. Besides the IPCC reports, Oreskes cites studies by the US National Academy of Sciences, the American Meteorological Society and the American Association for the Advancement of Science.

9   Oreskes, 'The Scientific Consensus on Climate Change: How Do We Know We're Not Wrong?', p. 73; she cites an earlier study which concluded that scientific consensus was reached as early as 1995. For contrarian views see B.J. Peiser, 'The Dangers of Consensus Science', Canada National Post, 17 May 2005; R.A. Pielke, 'Consensus About Climate Change?', Science, vol. 208, no. 5,724, pp. 952–3.

10 Peter T. Dornan and Maggie Kendall Zimmerman, 'Examining the Scientific Consensus on Climate Change', Eos, vol. 90, no. 3, 20 January 2009, pp. 22–3.

11 For a detailed discussion of scientific method in the context of climatology, see Oreskes, 'The Scientific Consensus on Climate Change: How Do We Know We're Not Wrong?', pp. 79–93. Even if there had been any validity behind the politically motivated and media-driven controversies that broke at the end of 2009 based on the wilful misinterpretation of stolen e-mails from a UK-based research unit and some insignificant errors in 4AR WG2, it would not have significantly damaged the scientific consensus.

12 'Climate Change: The Debate Heats Up', IISS Strategic Comments, vol. 13, no. 2, March 2007.

13 Ibid. The Third Assessment Report (TAR) is available at http://www1.ipcc.ch/ipccreports/assessments-reports.htm.

14 4AR WG1, p. 21 (TS), 95–121. The First Assessment Report was for the most part non-quantitative; the second report in 1995 found that the 'balance of evidence suggests a discernible human influence on global climate' and was instrumental in the successful negotiation of the Kyoto Protocol to the United Nations Framework Convention on Climate Change (UNFCCC).

15 Stephen McIntyre and Ross McKitrick, 'Corrections to the Mann et. al. (1998) Proxy Data Base and Northern Hemisphere Average Temperature Series', Energy and Environment, vol. 14, no. 6, November 2003, pp. 751–71; Hans von Storch et al., 'Reconstructing Past Climate from Noisy Data', Science, vol. 306, no. 5696, 22 October 2004, pp. 679–82; McIntyre and McKitrick, 'Hockey Sticks, Principal Components, and Spurious Significance', Geophysical Research Letters, vol. 32, L03710, 2005; Anders Moberg et al., 'Highly Variable Northern Hemisphere Temperatures Reconstructed from Low- and High-resolution Proxy Data', Nature, vol. 433, no. 7,026, 10 February 2005, pp. 613–17. Despite their concerns about some of the methods underlying the hockey stick, Moberg et al. actually reinforce and extend the main conclusions of that study.

16 Board on Atmospheric Sciences and Climate, Surface Temperature Reconstructions for the Past 2,000 Years (Washington DC: The National Academies Press, 2006); Edward J. Wegman et al., Ad Hoc Committee Report On The 'Hockey Stick' Global Climate Reconstruction, http://www.uoguelph.ca/~rmckitri/research/WegmanReport.pdf.

17 Stefan Rahmstorf, 'Testing Climate Reconstructions', Science, vol. 312, no. 5,782, 30 June 2006, p. 1,872; Eugene R. Wahl et al., 'Comment on "Reconstructing Past Climate from Noisy Data"', Science, vol. 312, no. 5,573, 26 April 2006, p. 529b; Wahl and Casper M. Ammann, 'Robustness of the Mann, Bradley, Hughes Reconstruction of Northern

Hemisphere Surface Temperatures: Examination of Criticisms Based on the Nature and Processing of Proxy Climate Evidence', *Climatic Change*, vol. 85, nos 1–2, November 2007, pp. 33–69; Ammann and Wahl, 'The Importance of the Geophysical Context in Statistical Evaluations of Climate Reconstruction Procedures', *Climatic Change*, vol. 85, nos 1–2, November 2007, pp. 71–88; Peter Huybers, 'Comment on "Hockey Sticks, Principal Components, and Spurious Significance" by McIntyre and McKitrick', *Geophysical Research Letters*, vol. 32, L20705, 2005, doi:10.1029/2005GL023395; von Storch and Eduardo. Zorita, 'Comment on "Hockey Sticks, Principal Components, and Spurious Significance" by McIntyre and McKitrick', *Geophysical Research Letters*, vol. 32, L20701, 2005; Mann et al., 'Proxy-based Reconstructions of Hemispheric and Global Surface Temperature Variations over the Past Two Millennia'.

18 4AR WG1, pp. 466–73.

19 See, for example, James Hansen et al., 'Target Atmospheric CO_2: Where Should Humanity Aim?', *Open Atmospheric Science Journal*, vol. 2, 2008, pp. 217–31, available at http://www.bentham.org/open/toascj/openaccess2.htm; Thomas R. Karl et al., *Weather and Climate Extremes in a Changing Climate. Regions of Focus: North America, Hawaii, Caribbean, and U.S. Pacific Islands*, Synthesis and Assessment Product 3.3 (Washington DC: US Climate Change Science Program, 2008), http://www.climatescience.gov/Library/sap/sap3-3/final-report/; Amanda Leigh Mascarelli, 'What We've Learned in 2008', *Nature Reports: Climate Change*, vol. 3, January 2009, pp. 4–6; Pew Center for Global Climate Change, *Key*

Scientific Developments since the IPCC Fourth Assessment Report, Science Brief 2, June 2009; Katherine Richardson et al., *Synthesis Report from Climate Change: Global Risks, Challenges & Decisions, Copenhagen 2009, 10–12 March* (Copenhagen: University of Copenhagen, 2009); I. Allison et al., *The Copenhagen Diagnosis: Updating the World on the Latest Climate Science* (Sydney: University of New South Wales Climate Change Research Centre, 2009).

20 4AR WG1, pp. 12 (SPM), 809.

21 4AR WG1, pp. 5, 12–13 (SPM). For the estimate of impacts see IPCC, *Climate Change 2007: Impacts, Adaptation and Vulnerability*, Working Group II Contribution to the Fourth Assessment Report (Cambridge: Cambridge University Press, 2007), p. 797, hereinafter 4AR WG2. It should be noted that this estimate is at low to medium confidence, but the impacts and level of confidence both increase with increasing temperatures.

22 For details see Chapter 4.

23 4AR WG1, p. 71 (TS).

24 4AR WG1, p. 13 (SPM).

25 4AR WG1, Table 11.1, pp. 854–7.

26 For methodological considerations relating to regional climate projections, see L.O. Mearns et al., 'Guidelines for Use of Climate Scenarios Developed from Regional Climate Model Experiments', 30 October 2003, http://www.ipcc-data.org/guidelines/dgm_no1_v1_10-2003.pdf; 4AR WG1, pp. 918–25.

27 See, for example, the summations in the synthesis and assessment products of the US Climate Change Science Program (CCSP), especially Karl et al., *Weather and Climate Extremes in a Changing Climate*; Paul van der

Linden and John F.B. Mitchell (eds), *ENSEMBLES: Climate Change and its Impacts: Summary of Research and Results from the ENSEMBLES Project* (Exeter: Met Office Hadley Centre, 2009), http://ensembles-eu.metoffice.com/docs/Ensembles_final_report_Nov09.pdf; Ross Garnaut, *The Garnaut Climate Change Review Final Report* (Cambridge: Cambridge University Press, 2008), http://www.garnautreview.org.au/. As of March 2010, the CCSP unified synthesis report was available in the form of the thirrd draft dated 27 April 2009, which is not intended for citation or quotation.

28 Richard Wood, 'Natural Ups and Downs', *Nature Reports Climate Change*, vol. 2, May 2008, p. 61.

29 N.S. Keenlyside et al., 'Advancing Decadal-scale Climate Prediction in the North Atlantic Sector', *Nature*, vol. 453, no. 7,191, 1 May 2008, pp. 84–9.

30 Doug M. Smith et al., 'Improved Surface Temperature Prediction for the Coming Decade from a Global Climate Model', *Science*, vol. 317, no. 5,839, 10 August 2007, pp. 796–9.

31 See Gerald A. Meehl, 'Decadal Prediction: Can It Be Skillful?', *Bulletin of the American Meteorological Society*, vol. 90, no. 10, October 2009, pp. 1,467–85.

32 4AR WG1, p. 809.

33 Ed Hawkins and Rowan Sutton, 'The Potential to Narrow Uncertainty in Regional Climate Predictions', *Bulletin of the American Meteorological Society*, vol. 90, no. 8, August 2009, pp. 1,095–1,107.

34 N. Nakićenović and R. Swart (eds), *IPCC Special Report on Emissions Scenarios* (Cambridge: Cambridge University Press, 2000). For a breakdown of the six scenarios used in the Fourth Assessment Report, see 4AR WG1, p. 18.

35 4AR WG2, pp. 146–7.

36 4AR WG1, p. 89 (TS).

37 David B. Lobell et al., 'Prioritizing Climate Change Adaptation Needs for Food Security in 2030', *Science*, vol. 319, no. 5,863, 1 February 2008, p. 608; 4AR WG1, p. 75 (TS).

38 *Ibid.*, p. 74.

39 UNFCCC, Article 2, http://unfccc.int/resource/docs/convkp/conveng.pdf.

40 See W. Neil Adger et al., 'Successful Adaptation to Climate Change Across Scales', *Global Environmental Change*, vol. 15, 2005, pp. 77–86.

41 4AR WG1, pp. 600–1; Oreskes, 'The Scientific Consensus on Climate Change: How Do We Know We're Not Wrong?', pp. 87–8.

42 For summaries of the projected physical, social and political impacts of anthropogenic climate change see Alan Dupont, *Climate Change and Security: Managing the Risk*, Report commissioned by the Garnaut Climate Change Review, June 2008, http://www.garnautreview.org.au/CA25734E0016A131/WebObj/05Security/$File/05%20Security.pdf; Dupont, 'The Strategic Implications of Climate Change', *Survival*, vol. 50, no. 3, June–July 2008, pp. 29–54; Herman and Treverton, 'The Political Consequences of Climate Change'; 'Climate Change: Security Implications and Regional Impacts', *Strategic Survey 2007*; 4AR WG1; WG2.

43 Burroughs, *Climate Change in Prehistory*, p. 5.

44 *Ibid.*, p. 298.

45 For details see 4AR WG1, pp. 818–19.

46 Timothy M. Lenton et al., 'Tipping Elements in the Earth's Climate

System', *Proceedings of the National Academy of Sciences*, vol. 105, no. 6, 12 Febrary 2008, pp. 1,786–93.

[47] IPCC 4AR, pp. 818–19.

[48] Diana Simpson, 'Climate Change and National Security', Muir S. Fairchild Research Information Center, Maxwell AFB, AL, April 2008, http://www.au.af. mil/au/aul/bibs/climate.htm.

[49] CNA Corporation, *National Security and the Threat of Climate Change*.

[50] 'Climate Change: Security Implications and Regional Impacts', *Strategic Survey 2007*.

[51] Campbell et al., *The Age of Consequences*, p. 6.

[52] Busby, *Climate Change and National Security*.

[53] Ben Russell and Nigel Morris, 'Armed Forces are Put on Standby to Tackle Threat of Wars over Water', *Independent*, 28 February 2006, http://news. independent.co.uk/environment/ article348196.ece.

[54] Ban Ki-moon, 'Secretary-General's Address to UNIS–UN Conference on Climate Change', http://www.un.org/ apps/sg/sgstats.asp?nid=2462.

[55] Beckett, 'Climate Change: "The Gathering Storm"'. For her remarks at the Security Council debate itself, see Beckett, 'Opening Remarks'.

[56] Council of the European Union, *Climate Change and International Security*; see also Nicole Itano, 'At EU Summit, Climate Change Billed as Major Security Risk', *Christian Science Monitor*, 14 March 2008, http://www. csmonitor.com/2008/0314/p06s01- wogn.html?page=1.

[57] 'France Warns Climate Change Driving War, Hunger', AFP, 18 April 2008.

[58] 'Expert: Climate Change Could Mean "Extended World War"', AP, 23 February 2009.

[59] Ban Ki-moon, 'A Climate Culprit in Darfur', *Washington Post*, 16 June 2007, p. A15.

[60] See Stephan Faris, 'The Real Roots of Darfur', *The Atlantic*, April 2007, http://www.theatlantic.com/doc/ print/200704/darfur-climate.

[61] Alex de Waal, 'Is Climate Change the Culprit for Darfur?', SSRC Blogs, Climate and Environment: Making Sense of Darfur, http://www.ssrc.org/ blogs/darfur/2007/06/25/is-climate- change-the-culprit-for-darfur/.

[62] Michael Kevane and Leslie Gray, 'Darfur: Rainfall and Conflict', *Environmental Research Letters*, vol. 3, 2008, 034006.

[63] William H. McNeill, *Plagues and Peoples* (New York: Anchor Books, 1976), pp. 82–90.

[64] *Ibid.*, pp. 90–4.

[65] James C. McCann, 'Climate and Causation in African History', *International Journal of African Historical Studies*, vol. 32, 1999, pp. 261–79, available at http://www.h-net. org/~environ/historiography/africa. htm.

[66] Jared Diamond, *Guns, Germs and Steel: The Fates of Human Societies* (New York: W.W. Norton, 1997).

[67] See J. Donald Hughes, *An Environmental History of the World: Humankind's Changing Role in the Community of Life* (London and New York: Routledge, 2001), pp. 52–79.

[68] Ellsworth Huntington, *The Pulse of Asia: A Journey in Central Asia Illustrating the Geographical Basis of History* (Boston, MA: Houghton, Mifflin and Co., 1907); Huntington, *Civilization and Climate* (New Haven, CT: Yale University Press, 1915).

[69] See David Herlihy, 'Ecological Conditions and Demographic Change',

in Richard L. DeMolen (ed.), *One Thousand Years: Western Europe in the Middle Ages* (Boston, MA: Houghton Mifflin, 1974), pp. 6–7. Herlihy offers a good, if dated, survey of the influence of environmental factors on the history of Western Europe. See also John E. Chappell, Jr, 'Climatic Change Reconsidered: Another Look at "The Pulse of Asia"', *Geographical Review*, vol. 60, no. 3, July 1970, pp. 347–73.

[70] Halford J. Mackinder, 'The Geographical Pivot of History', *Geographical Journal*, vol. 23, 1904, pp. 421–37.

[71] Schubert et al., *Climate Change as a Security Risk*, pp. 25–9. The authors also discuss a fourth, more recent approach from the Irvine group, which is less a coherent methodology than a call for reorienting research towards issues of human security, and the 'syndrome-based' approach developed under the auspices of the WBGU itself.

[72] *Ibid.*, p. 30.

[73] See Thomas Homer-Dixon, 'Strategies for Studying Causation in Complex Ecological Political Systems', Occasional Paper, Projected on Environment, Population and Security, American Association for the Advancement of Science and the University of Toronto, June 1995, available at http://www.library.utoronto.ca/pcs/eps/method/methods1.htm; Charles C. Ragin, *The Comparative Method: Moving Beyond Qualitative and Quantitative Strategies* (Berkeley and Los Angeles, CA: University of California Press, 1987).

[74] Schubert at al., *Climate Change as a Security Risk*.

[75] Martin McCauley, *The Rise and Fall of the Soviet Union* (Harlow: Pearson Education, 2008), pp. 147, 252.

[76] For further discussion on this point see Jeffrey Mazo, 'Failure is No Success at All', *Survival*, vol. 47, no. 3, Autumn 2005, pp. 165–72.

Chapter Two

[1] See Diamond, *Guns, Germs and Steel* and McNeill, *Plagues and Peoples*, both discussed in Chapter One; see also Burroughs, *Climate Change in Prehistory*, pp. 276–81.

[2] Diamond, *Guns, Germs and Steel*, pp. 46–7.

[3] For a general survey see Brian Fagan, *The Long Summer: How Climate Changed Civilization* (London: Granta, 2004), pp. 68–78.

[4] See *ibid.*, pp. 57, 79–96; Burroughs, *Climate Change in Prehistory*, pp. 188–92.

[5] See Fagan, *The Long Summer*, pp. 107–10; Burroughs, *Climate Change in Prehistory*, pp. 57–63, 218–20; Laura Spinney, 'In Search of the Missing Stone Age Tribes', *New Scientist*, 8 November 2008, pp. 40–3.

[6] See Fagan, *The Long Summer*, pp. 111–15; Burroughs, *Climate Change in Prehistory*, pp. 220–2. Burroughs presents the more balanced discussion of the somewhat controversial evidence for the Euxine flood.

[7] Paul A. Mayewski et al., 'Holocene Climate Variability', *Quarternary Research*, vol. 62, 2004, pp. 243–56. Mayewski and colleagues draw on around 50 different climate proxies

from around the world. Because of regional climate differences and sensitivity of the proxies, not every rapid climate-change event is reflected in every record. The 'hockey-stick controversy' discussed in Chapter One demonstrates some of the difficulties of reconstructing past temperatures, but it is past climates that are important in this context, and the proxies used to reconstruct temperatures are direct indicators of climate. Variation in global mean temperature, as a driver of climate change more broadly, is important when making future projections or predictions, but less so for analysis of the historical interaction between climate and culture.

8   4AR WG1, p. 435; see also pp. 459–65.

9   Heinz Wanner et al., 'Mid- to Late Holocene Climate Change: An Overview', *Quarternary Science Reviews*, vol. 27, 2008, pp. 1,791–828, using a smaller set of 18 proxy series, fail to find evidence of any rapid climate-change events on a global scale over the last 6,000 years.

10   See David G. Anderson et al., 'Climate and Culture Change: Exploring Holocene Transitions', in Anderson et al. (eds), *Climate Change and Cultural Dynamics: A Global Perspective on Mid-Holocene Transitions* (London: Academic Press, 2007), pp. 12–18; the various other essays in that volume; Raven Garvey et al., 'Middle Holocene Behavioural Strategies in the Americas', *Before Farming*, no. 2, 2008, article 1, http://www.waspjournals.com/journals/beforefarming/journal_20082/abstracts/index.php; Gustavo Neme and Adolfo Gil, 'Human Occupation and Increasing Mid-Holocene Aridity', *Current Anthropology*, vol. 50, no. 1, February 2009, pp. 149–63; Nick Brooks,

'Cultural Responses to Aridity in the Middle Holocene and Increased Social Complexity', *Quarternary International*, vol. 151, 2006, pp. 29–49.

11   For the most recent and detailed reconstruction of mean global temperatures over the last 2,000 years see Mann et al., 'Proxy-based Reconstructions of Hemispheric and Global Surface Temperature Variations over the Past Two Millennia'.

12   Unless otherwise indicated, details of Easter Island's history, society and ecology follow Diamond, *Collapse: How Societies Choose to Fail or Survive* (London: Penguin, 2005), pp. 79–119.

13   Mayewski et al., 'Holocene Climate Variability', p. 251–2

14   Diamond, *Collapse*, pp. 115–18.

15   Mayweski et al., 'Holocene Climate Variability', p. 250.

16   Brooks, 'Beyond Collapse: The Role of Climatic Dessication in the Emergence of Complex Societies in the Middle Holocene', in S. Leroy and P. Costa (eds), *Environmental Catastrophes in Mauritania, the Desert and the Coast*, Abstract Volume and Field Guide, First Joint Meeting of ICSU Dark Nature and IGCP490, 4–18 January 2004, Mauritania, pp. 26–30, available at http://www.nickbrooks.org/publications/Brooks-BeyondCollapse-abs.pdf; Brooks, 'Cultural Responses to Aridity in the Middle Holocene and Increased Social Complexity'; Anderson et al., *Climate Change and Cultural Dynamics* and other essays contained in that volume.

17   See Fagan, *The Long Summer*, pp. 128–45; Burroughs, *Climate Change in Prehistory*, pp. 240–55.

18   Harvey Weiss et al., 'The Genesis and Collapse of Third Millennium North Mesopotamian Civilization', *Science*,

vol. 261, no. 5,124, 20 August 1993, pp. 995–1,004; Weiss, 'Beyond the Younger Dryas: Collapse as Adaptation to Abrupt Climate Change in Ancient West Asia and the Eastern Mediterranean', in Garth Bawden and Richard Martin Reycraft (eds), *Environmental Disaster and the Archaeology of Human Response*, Anthropological Papers no. 7 (Albuquerque, NM: Maxwell Museum of Anthropology, 2000), pp. 75–98; Richard A. Kerr, 'Sea-Floor Dust Shows Drought Felled Akkadian Empire', *Science*, vol. 279, no. 5,349, 16 January 1998, pp. 325–6; H.M. Cullen et al., 'Climate Change and the Collapse of the Akkadian Empire: Evidence from the Deep Sea', *Geology*, vol. 28, no. 4, April 2000, pp. 379–82; Peter B. deMenocal, 'Cultural Responses to Climate Change During the Late Holocene', *Science*, vol. 292, no. 5,517, 27 April 2001, p. 669; L. Ristvet, 'Agriculture, Settlement, and Abrupt Climate Change: The 4.2ka BP Event in Northern Mesopotamia', *Eos*, vol. 89, no. 53, 2003, Fall Meeting Supplement, Abstract, PP22C-02, http://adsabs.harvard.edu/abs/2003AGUFMPP22C.02R.

[19] N. Catto and G. Catto, 'Climate Change, Communities, and Civilizations: Driving Force, Supporting Player, or Background Noise?', *Quarternary International*, vol. 123–5, 2004, pp. 7–10.

[20] For a view that rapid climate change and its social impacts at this time were limited to southwest Asia and Egypt, see Burroughs, *Climate Change in Prehistory*, pp. 254–5.

[21] Mayewski et al., 'Holocene Climate Variability'.

[22] Catto and Catto, 'Climate Change, Communities, and Civilizations: Driving Force, Supporting Player, or Background Noise?'; M. Staubwasser et al., 'Climate Change at the 4.2 ka BP Termination of the Indus Valley Civilization and Holocene South Asian Monsoon Variability', *Geophysical Research Letters*, vol. 30, no. 8, 2003.

[23] Marco Madella and Dorian Q. Fuller, 'Paleoecology and the Harappan Civilisation of South Asia: A Reconsideration', *Quarternary Science Reviews*, vol. 25, 2006, pp. 1,283–1,301.

[24] Wu Wenxiang and Liu Tungsheng, 'Possible Role of the "Holocene Event 3" on the Collapse of Neolithic Cultures around the Central Plain of China', *Quaternary International*, vol. 117, no. 1, 2004, pp. 153–66; Gao Huazhong et al., 'Environmental Change and Cultural Response around 4200 cal. yr BP in the Yishu River Basin, Shandong', *Journal of Geographical Sciences*, vol. 17, no. 3, July 2007, pp. 285–92.

[25] Burroughs, *Climate Change in Prehistory*, pp. 256–8; Fagan, *The Long Summer*, pp. 178–88.

[26] Carole L. Crumley, 'Analyzing Historic Ecotonal Shifts', *Ecological Applications*, vol. 3, no. 3, 1993, pp. 377–84.

[27] Eelco J. Rohling et al., 'Holocene Climate Variability in the Eastern Mediterranean, and the End of the Bronze Age', in C. Bachhuber and G. Roberts (eds), *Forces of Transformation: The End of the Bronze Age in the Mediterranean* (Oxford: Oxbow, 2009), preprint available at http://www.noc.soton.ac.uk/soes/staff/ejr/Rohling-papers/2008-Rohling et al Oxbow chapter FINAL.pdf.

[28] See Joseph A. Tainter, *The Collapse of Complex Societies* (Cambridge: Cambridge University Press, 1988), pp. 148–50.

[29] Fagan, *The Long Summer*, pp. 200–7.

[30] Tainter, *The Collapse of Complex Societies*, p. 151.

31 Burroughs, *Does the Weather Really Matter? The Social Implications of Climate Change* (Cambridge: Cambridge University Press, 1997), p. 20.

32 4AR WG1, pp. 468–9; Fagan, *The Long Summer*, pp. 211–12; Burroughs, *Does the Weather Really Matter?*, pp. 107–9; Mann et al., 'Global Signatures and Dynamical Origins of the Little Ice Age and Medieval Climate Anomaly', *Science*, vol. 326. no. 5,957, 27 November 2009, pp. 1,256–60.

33 Herlihy, 'Ecological Conditions and Demographic Change'.

34 Burroughs, *Does the Weather Really Matter?*, pp. 34–42, 109–12; Christian Pfister, 'Climatic Extremes, Recurrent Crises and Witch Hunts: Strategies of European Societies in Coping with Exogenous Shocks in the Late Sixteenth and Early Seventeenth Centuries', *Medieval History Journal*, vol. 10, nos 1–2, 2007, pp. 33–73; Fagan, *The Long Summer*, pp. 248–50; Wolfgang Behringer, *A Cultural History of Climate* (London: Polity, 2010); Herlihy, *The Black Death and the Transformation of the West* (Cambridge, MA: Harvard University Press, 1997).

35 Pingzhong Zhang et al., 'A Test of Climate, Sun, and Culture Relationships from an 1810-Year Chinese Cave Record', *Science*, vol. 322, no. 5,903, 7 November 2008, pp. 940–42.

36 Harry F. Lee et al., 'Climatic Change and Chinese Population Growth Dynamics over the Last Millenium', *Climatic Change*, vol. 88, 2008, pp. 131–56.

37 David D. Zhang et al., 'Climate Change and War Frequency in Eastern China over the Last Millenium', *Human Ecology*, vol. 35, no. 4, pp. 403–14

38 Victor J. Polyak and Yemane Asmerom, 'Late Holocene Climate and Cultural Changes in the Southwestern United States', *Science*, vol. 294, no. 5,540, 5 October 2001, pp. 148–51; Mark Brenner et al., 'Abrupt Climate Change and Pre-Columbian Cultural Collapse', in Vera Markgraff (ed.), *Interhemispheric Climate Linkages* (London: Academic Press, 2001), pp. 87–102; deMenocal, 'Cultural Responses to Climate Change During the Late Holocene'; Terry L. Jones and Al Schwitalla, 'Archaeological Perspectives on the Effects of Medieval Drought in Prehistoric California', *Quarternary International*, vol. 188, no. 1, September 2008, pp. 41–58; Michael W. Binford et al., 'Climate Variation and the Rise and Fall of an Andean Civilisation', *Quarternary Research*, vol. 47, no. 2, March 1997, pp. 235–48; Diamond, *Collapse*, pp. 136–56; Henry F. Diaz and David W. Stahle, 'Climate and Cultural History in the Americas: An Overview', *Climatic Change*, vol. 83, no. 1, July 2007, pp. 1–8.

39 See Diamond, *Collapse*, pp. 157–77; Fagan, *The Long Summer*, pp. 229–38, esp. p. 236; deMenocal, 'Cultural Responses to Climate Change During the Late Holocene'.

40 Diamond, *Guns, Germs and Steel*, esp. pp. 344–60.

41 McNeill, *Plagues and Peoples*, pp. 188–90; Diamond, *Guns, Germs and Steel*, pp. 210–12. McNeill's estimate of 100m for the total New World population is now generally considered too high.

42 R.J. Nevle and D.K. Bird, 'Effects of Syn-pandemic Fire Reduction and Reforestation in the Tropical Americas on Atmospheric Carbon Dioxide During European Conquest', *Eos*, vol. 89, no. 53, Fall Meeting Supplement, abstract U31A-0004; Stanford University News Service, 'Post-pandemic Reforestation in New World Helped Trigger Little

Ice Age, Stanford Researchers Say', press release, 18 December 2008, http://news-service.stanford.edu/pr/2008/pr-manvleaf-010709.html.

43 Thomas B. van Hoof et al., 'Forest Re-growth on Medieval Farmland after the Black Death Pandemic: Implications for Atmospheric CO_2 Levels', *Palaeogeography, Palaeoclimatology, Palaeoecology*, vol. 237, nos. 2–4, August 2006, pp. 396–409.

44 Burroughs, *Does the Weather Really Matter?*, pp. 45–50; US National Drought Mitigation Center, 'Drought in the Dust Bowl Years', 2006, http://drought.unl.edu/whatis/dustbowl.htm.

45 DeMenocal, 'Cultural Responses to Climate Change During the Late Holocene'; Richard Seager et al., 'The Characteristics and Likely Causes of the Medieval Megadroughts in North America', Lamont-Doherty Earth Observatory Research Paper, 2007, http://www.ldeo.columbia.edu/res/div/ocp/drought/medieval.shtml; K.R. Laird et al., 'Greater Drought Intensity and Frequency before AD 1200 in the Northern Great Plains, USA', *Nature*, vol. 384, pp. 552–4; Siegfried D. Schubert et al., 'On the Cause of the 1930s Dust Bowl', *Science*, vol. 303, no. 5,665, 19 March 2004, pp. 1855–9; Benjamin I. Cook et al., 'Amplification of the North American "Dust Bowl" Drought through Human-induced Land Degradation', *Proceedings of the National Academy of Sciences*, vol. 106, no. 13, 31 March 2009, pp. 4,997–5,001.

46 Robert Strayer, *Why Did the Soviet Union Collapse: Understanding Historical Change* (London: M.E. Sharpe, 1988).

47 Diamond, *Collapse*, p. 11.

48 *Ibid.*, pp. 311–28; quotation at p. 313.

49 *Ibid.*, pp. 329–57.

50 *Ibid.*, pp. 154–5.

51 Burroughs, *Climate Change in Prehistory*, pp. 270–4.

52 Brooks, 'Beyond Collapse: The Role of Climatic Dessication in the Emergence of Complex Societies in the Middle Holocene'; Fagan, *The Long Summer*; Brooks, 'Cultural Responses to Aridity in the Middle Holocene and Increased Social Complexity', p. 45.

53 Burroughs, *Climate Change in Prehistory*, p. 274.

54 Anderson et al., 'Climate and Culture Change', p. 12.

55 Brooks, 'Beyond Collapse'; Brooks, 'Cultural Responses to Aridity in the Middle Holocene and Increased Social Complexity'.

56 *Ibid.*, p. 38.

57 Weiss, 'Beyond the Younger Dryas'.

58 Fagan, *The Long Summer*, p. 87.

59 Madella and Fuller, 'Paleoecology and the Harappan Civilisation of South Asia'.

60 Charles Keith Maisels, *Early Civilisations of the Old World* (London: Routledge, 1999), pp. 252–5.

61 See Diamond, *Collapse*, pp. 136–56; Fagan, *The Long Summer*, pp. 211, 226–8; Seager et al., 'The Characteristics and Likely Causes of the Medieval Megadroughts in North America'.

62 See Ole Waever, 'Security Implications of Climate Change', in Katherine Richardson et al., *Synthesis Report from Climate Change: Global Risks, Challenges & Decisions, Copenhagen 2009, 10–12 March* (Copenhagen: University of Copenhagen, 2009), p. 17.

63 For a detailed discussion see Diamond, *Collapse*, pp. 427–31.

64 See *ibid.*, p. 433.

65 See *ibid.*, pp. 434–6.

66 Burroughs, *Climate Change in Prehistory*, pp. 47–9.

67 Alistair Moffat, *Before Scotland: The Story of Scotland Before History* (London: Thames & Hudson, 2005), pp. 170, 177.

68 Thorvaldur Thordarson and Stephen Self, 'Atmospheric and Environmental Effects of the 1783–1784 Laki Eruption: A Review and Reassessment', *Journal of Geophysical Research*, vol. 108, no. D1, 4011, doi: 10.1029.2001JD002042, 2003; Stephen Sparks et al., *Super-eruptions: Global Effects and Future Threats*, Report of a Geological Society of London Working Group, 2nd (print) ed., 2005, p. 11.

69 Helgi Skuli Kjartansson, 'The Onset of Emigration from Iceland', *American Studies in Scandinavia*, vol. 10, no. 1, 1977, pp. 87–93.

70 See Burroughs, *Climate Change in Prehistory*, pp. 54–72.

71 See, for example, Benny Peiser, 'Climate Change and Civilisation Collapse', in Kendra Okonski (ed.), *Adapt or Die: The Science, Politics and Economics of Climate Change* (London: Profile, 2003), pp. 191–204.

72 Zhang et al., 'Climate Change and War Frequency in Eastern China over the Last Millenium'.

73 Chen Fahu et al., 'Humid Little Ice Age in Arid Central Asia Documented by Bosten Lake, Xinjinag, China', *Science in China Series D: Earth Sciences*, vol. 49, no. 12, 2006, pp. 1,280–90.

74 David D. Zhang et al., 'Global Climate Change, War, and Population Decline in Recent Human History', *Proceedings of the National Academy of Sciences*, vol. 104, no. 49, 4 December 2007, pp. 19,214–19.

75 Richard S.J. Tol and Sebastian Wagner, 'Climate Change and Violent Conflict in Europe over the Last Millennium', *Climatic Change*, published online 30 September 2009, doi: 10.1007/s10584-009-9659-2.

Chapter Three

1 'Sudan (Darfur): Historical Background)', IISS *Armed Conflict Database* (ACD), http://www.iiss.org/publications/armed-conflict-database/.

2 United Nations Environment Programme, *Sudan: Post-conflict Environment Assessment* (Nairobi: UNEP, 2007), p. 75.

3 Ban Ki-moon, 'A Climate Culprit in Darfur'.

4 For a transcript see http://forumpolitics.com/blogs/2007/03/17/an-inconvient-truth-transcript/.

5 Paul Reynolds, 'Security Council Takes on Global Warming', BBC News, 18 April 2007, http://news.bbc.co.uk/1/hi/world/americas/6559211.stm.

6 'Sudan – Complex Emergency', USAID Situation Report no. 4, 5 February 2010, http://www.usaid.gov/locations/sub-saharan_africa/sudan/.

7 Gérard Prunier, *Darfur: The Ambiguous Genocide* (London: Hurst, 2005), p. 4; ACD, 'Sudan (Darfur): Historical Background'; Bakri Osman Saeed, 'Preface', in *Environmental Degradation as a Cause of Conflict in Darfur, Conference Proceedings, Khartoum, December 2004* (Addis Ababa: University for Peace Africa Programme, 2006), p. 8.

8   Prunier, *Darfur: The Ambiguous Genocide*, p. 5; Saeed, 'Preface', p. 8.

9   Abduljabbar Abdalla Fadul, 'Natural Resources Management for Sustainable Peace in Darfur', in *Environmental Degradation as a Cause of Conflict in Darfur*, p. 42.

10 Nick Brooks, 'Climate Change, Drought and Pastoralism in the Sahel', discussion note for the World Initiative on Sustainable Pastoralism, November 2006, available at http://nickbrooks.org/publications/WISP_CCAP_Find_en_v2.pdf

11 Nick Brooks, 'Drought in the African Sahel: Long Term Perspectives and Future Prospects', Tyndall Centre Working Paper No. 61, October 2004, http://www.tyndall.ac.uk/publications/working_papers/wp61.pdf, pp. 5–7; McCann, 'Climate and Causation in African History'; A. Mayor et al., 'Population Dynamics and Paleoclimate over the Past 3000 Years in the Dogon Country, Mali', *Journal of Anthropological Archaeology*, vol. 24, 2005, pp. 25–61.

12 UNEP, *Sudan: Post-Conflict Environment Assessment*, p. 59; Kevane and Gray, 'Darfur: Rainfall and Conflict', p. 2.

13 Brooks, 'Drought in the African Sahel: Long Term Perspectives and Future Prospects', pp. 1–2. Brooks's data run to 2002.

14 Wassila M. Thiaw, 'Recent Climate Anomalies in the Sahel: Natural Variability or Climate Change?, *CLIVAR Focus on Africa*, http://www.clivar.org/organization/vacs/docs/Sahel3.pdf, p. 1.

15 *Ibid.*; Brooks, 'Drought in the African Sahel: Long Term Perspectives and Future Prospects', pp. 19–20; 4AR WG1, p. 866.

16 Kevane and Gray, 'Darfur: Rainfall and Conflict', p. 6.

17 Christian Webersik, 'Sudan Climate Change and Security Factsheet', United Nations University Institute of Advanced Studies, Climate Change Facts Sheets Series 2008/2, http://www.ias.unu.edu/resource_centre/Sudan_Climate Change Facts Sheets Series_2008_2_lowres.pdf, p. 2 (Fig. 2); http://www.yale.edu/gsp/gis-files/darfur/abstract_veg_increases.html.

18 'Long-term Increases in Vegetation Accompanying the Genocide in Darfur, 2003–2007', Yale University Genocide Studies Program, http://www.yale.edu/gsp/gis-files/darfur/abstract_veg_increases.html.

19 UNEP, *Sudan: Post-Conflict Environment Assessment*, pp. 81–2, citing a 2003 study.

20 For details of the local conflict-resolution mechanisms and institutions, see Yagoub Abdalla Mohamed, 'Land Tenure, Land use and Conflicts in Darfur', in Environmental Degradation as a Cause of Conflict in Darfur, pp. 59–68.

21 R.S. O'Fahey, 'Conflict in Darfur: Historical and Contemporary Perspectives', in *Environmental Degradation as a Cause of Conflict in Darfur*, p. 26.

22 *Ibid.*, p. 42.

23 UNEP, *Sudan: Post-Conflict Environment Assessment*, pp. 81–3.

24 'Sudan (SPLM/A and NDA): Historical Background', ACD; 'Sudan (Darfur): Historical Background', ACD.

25 Prunier, *Darfur: The Ambiguous Genocide*, pp. 47–56.

26 'Sudan (Darfur): Historical Background', ACD.

27 Prunier, *Darfur: The Ambiguous Genocide*, pp. 74–5.

28 Kevane and Gray, 'Darfur: Rainfall and Conflict', quotation at p. 8.

29 Marshall B. Burke et al., 'Warming Increases the Risk of Civil War in Africa', *Proceedings of the National Academy of Sciences*, vol. 106, no. 49, 8 December 2009, pp. 20,670–74. Temperature data were not available to Kevane and Gray; Kevane subsequently acknowledged the difference between the temperature trend and precipitation step change, although he had reservations about the adequacy of the data for small-scale regional analysis. Michael Kevane; 'Two Graphs of Rainfall and Temperature in Darfur', Understanding Sudan: Commentary, http://sudancommentary.blogspot.com/2009/11/two-graphs-of-rainfall-and-temperature.

30 Mike De Souza, 'Darfur War, Climate Change Linked', *Ottawa Citizen*, 17 April 2007, http://www2.canada.com/ottawacitizen/news/story.html?id=875bb083-b8c1-4178-9518-db3e5216a903.

31 CNA Corporation, *National Security and the Threat of Climate Change*, p. 16.

32 Tor A. Benjaminsen, 'Does Supply-Induced Scarcity Drive Violent Conflicts in the African Sahel? The Case of the Tuareg Rebellion in Northern Mali', *Journal of Peace Research*, vol. 45, no. 6, 2008, pp. 819–36.

33 4AR WG1, p. 299.

34 Kevane and Gray, 'Darfur: Rainfall and Conflict', p. 2.

35 *Ibid.*, pp. 2, 5; UNEP, *Sudan: Post-Conflict Environment Assessment*, p. 82.

36 The discussion in the next two paragraphs follows de Waal, 'Is Climate Change the Culprit for Darfur?', unless otherwise indicated.

37 Mary E. King and Mohamed Awad Oswan, 'Executive Summary', in *Environmental Degradation as a Cause of Conflict in Darfur*, p. 20; O'Fahey, 'Conflict in Darfur: Historical and Contemporary Perspectives', p. 25.

38 A. Gianni et al., 'Oceanic Forcing of Sahel Rainfall on Interannual to Interdecadal Timescales', *Science*, vol. 306, no. 5,647, 7 November 2003, pp. 1,027–30; John C. Fyfe, 'Extratropical Southern Hemisphere Cyclones: Harbingers of Climate Change?', *Journal of Climate*, vol. 16, no. 17, September 2003, pp. 2,802–5; Brooks, 'Drought in the African Sahel: Long Term Perspectives and Future Prospects', pp. 9–22; Flannery, *The Weather Makers*, p. 124; 4AR WG1, p. 715.

39 4AR WG1, p. 256, 299.

40 Homer-Dixon, 'Cause and Effect', SSRC Blogs, Climate and Environment: Making Sense of Darfur, http://www.ssrc.org/blogs/darfur/2007/08/02/cause-and-effect (emphasis added).

41 *Ibid.*

42 De Waal, 'Response to "Cause and Effect"', SSRC Blogs, Climate and Environment: Making Sense of Darfur, http://www.ssrc.org/blogs/darfur/2007/08/02/cause-and-effect.

43 UNEP, *Sudan: Post-Conflict Environment Assessment*, p. 78.

44 *Ibid.*, p. 80.

45 *Ibid.*, p. 83.

46 *Ibid.*, pp. 88, 95.

Chapter Four

1   *The National Security Strategy of the United States of America*, The White House, September 2002, p. 4, http://georgewbush-whitehouse.archives.gov/nsc/nss/2002/nss.pdf; *The National Security Strategy of the United States of America*, The White House, March 2006, p. 15, available at http://www.comw.org/qdr/fulltext/nss2006.pdf.

2   See Robert I. Rotberg, 'Failed States in a World of Terror', *Foreign Affairs*, vol. 81, no. 4, July–August 2002, pp. 127–40; Rotberg (ed.), *When States Fail: Causes and Consequences* (Princeton, NJ: Princeton University Press, 2004); European Report on Development, *Development in a Context of Fragility: Focus on Africa*, outline report, 13 February 2009, http://ec.europa.eu/development/icenter/repository/ERD-Outline-Report-13-02-2009_en.pdf, pp. 18–24. For syntheses of theoretical and definitional issues surrounding state fragility and failure, see Claire Mcloughlin, *Fragile States*, Governance and Social Development Resource Centre Topic Guide (Birmingham: International Development Department, University of Birmingham, 2009), http://www.gsdrc.org/docs/open/CON67.pdf; and Robert B. Zoellick, 'Fragile States: Securing Development', *Survival*, vol. 50, no. 6, December 2008–January 2009, pp. 67–84.

3   Rotberg, 'The New Nature of Nation-State Failure', *Washington Quarterly*, vol. 25, no. 3, Summer 2002, pp. 90–3.

4   Foreign Policy and the Fund for Peace, 'The Failed States Index 2009', *Foreign Policy*, July–August 2009, pp. 80–93, http://www.foreignpolicy.com/articles/2009/06/22/the_2009_failed_states_index; Country Indicators for Foreign Policy, Carleton University, Fragile and Failed States Project, http://www.carleton.ca/cifp/ffs.htm; Susan E. Rice and Stewart Patrick, *Index of State Weakness in the Developing World* (Washington DC: Brookings Institution, 2008), http://www.brookings.edu/reports/2008/02_weak_states_index.aspx.

5   See, for example, the CIFP Conflict Risk Assessment project, http://www.carleton.ca/cifp/cra.htm; and the Political Instability Task Force models, http://globalpolicy.gmu.edu/pitf/.

6   Tainter, *The Collapse of Complex Societies*, pp. 121–2.

7   *Ibid.*, p. 206.

8   See 4AR WG2, pp. 821–4.

9   Diamond, *Collapse*, p. 420. For Tainter's response to Diamond see Peter B. deMenocal et al., 'Perspectives on Diamond's *Collapse: How Societies Choose to Fail or Succeed*', *Current Anthropology*, vol. 46, suppl., December 2005, pp. S91–S99.

10   Tainter, *The Collapse of Complex Societies*, p. 213.

11   *Ibid.*, pp. 213–14.

12   *Ibid.*, p. 214.

13   Rotberg, 'The New Nature of Nation-State Failure', p. 93.

14   4AR WG1, pp. 16(SPM); 74 (TS); WG2, pp. 175, 183–90.

15   Brian Hoyle, 'The Energy–Water Nexus: Deja-vu All Over Again?', *Nature Reports Climate Change*, vol. 2, April 2008, pp. 46–7.

16   Bryson Bates et al. (eds), *Climate Change and Water*, IPCC Technical Paper (Geneva: Intergovernmental Panel on Climate Change, 2008).

17   4AR WG2, pp. 444–5; Bates et al., *Climate Change and Water*, pp. 81–2.

18 4AR WG2, p. 54.

19 *Ibid.*, p. 598.

20 *Ibid.*, p. 471.

21 Bates et al., *Climate Change and Water*, p. 87.

22 4AR WG2, pp. 11–12 (SPM).

23 *Ibid.*, p. 275.

24 *Ibid.*, p. 299, Table 5.6.

25 Nigel W. Arnell, 'Climate Change and Water Resources: A Global Perspective', in Hans Joachim Schellnhuber et al. (eds), *Avoiding Dangerous Climate Change* (Cambridge: Cambridge University Press, 2006), pp. 167–75.

26 Josef Schmidhuber and Francesco N. Tubiello, 'Global Food Security under Climate Change', *Proceedings of the National Academy of Sciences*, vol. 104, no. 50, 11 December 2007, pp. 19,703–8.

27 Molly E. Brown and Christopher C. Funk, 'Food Security Under Climate Change', *Science*, vol. 319, no. 5,863, 1 February 2008, pp. 580–81; 4AR WG2, pp. 275–6.

28 *Ibid.*, pp. 328–33.

29 *Ibid.*, pp. 302, 448.

30 *Ibid.*, pp. 583, 597.

31 *Ibid.*, pp. 597.

32 *Ibid.*, pp. 471, 482–3. The crop yield and risk hunger projections are not strictly comparable since they are based on different emissions scenarios.

33 Lobell et al., 'Prioritizing Climate Change Adaptation Needs for Food Security in 2030'.

34 Burroughs, *Climate Change in Prehistory*, p. 296.

35 4AR WG2, p. 375.

36 Burroughs (ed.), *Climate into the 21st Century* (Cambridge: Cambridge University Press for the World Meteorological Organisation, 2003), pp. 109–10.

37 4AR WG2, p. 813.

38 *Ibid.*

39 Melissa Dell et al., 'Climate Shocks and Economic Growth: Evidence from the Last Half Century', paper presented at the American Economics Association Annual Meeting, San Francsisco, CA, 3–7 January 2009, available at http://www.aeaweb.org/annual_mtg_papers/2009/retrieve.php?pdfid=218.

40 4AR WG2, p. 365; Anna Barnett, 'Report Disperses Migration Myth', *Nature Reports Climate Change*, vol. 3, July 2009, pp. 79–80; Sabine L. Perch-Nielsen et al., 'Exploring the Link between Climate Change and Migration', *Climatic Change*, vol. 91, nos 3–4, December 2008, pp. 375–93.

41 Gaia Vince, 'Coping with Climate Change: Which Societies Will Do Best?', *Yale Environment 360*, 2 November 2009, http://www.e360.yale.edu/content/feature.msp?id=2205.

42 Brooks et al., 'The Determinants of Vulnerability and Adaptive Capacity at the National Level and the Implications for Adaptation', *Global Environmental Change*, vol. 15, 2005, pp. 151–61.

43 Vince, 'Coping with Climate Change: Which Societies Will Do Best?'.

44 Burroughs, *Climate Change in Prehistory*, p. 295.

45 'How Equine Flu brought the US to a Standstill', *Horsetalk*, 26 September 2007, http://www.horsetalk.co.nz/features/equineflu-131.shtml.

46 Alan Dupont and Mark Thirlwell, 'Are We Entering a New Era of Food Insecurity?', *Survival*, vol. 51, no. 3, June–July 2009, pp. 71–98.

47 International Energy Agency, *World Energy Outlook 2009* (Paris: IEA, 2009).

48 For a discussion of these variables in a broader context see W. Neil Adger, 'Social and Ecological Resilance: Are

they Related?', *Progress in Human Geography*, vol. 24, no. 3, 2000, pp. 347–64, TAR, p. 995.

49 Brooks et al., 'The Determinants of Vulnerability and Adaptive Capacity at the National Level and the Implications for Adaptation'.

50 ECOWAS-SWAC/OECD, 'Climate and Climate Change', *Atlas on Regional Integration in West Africa* (Paris: ECOWAS-SWAC/OECD, 2008), p. 13.

51 Burke et al., 'Warming Increases the Risk of Civil War in Africa'.

52 4AR WG2, p. 854.

53 Oli Brown and Alex Crawford, *Assessing the Security Implications of Climate Change for West Africa: Country Case Studies of Ghana and Burkina Faso* (Winnipeg, MB: International Institute for Sustainable Development, 2008), pp. viii–ix.

54 United Nations Association of Iran, *Climate Change and Iran*, UNA-Iran Report, April 2008, available at http://www.unairan.org; A. Koocheki et al., 'Potential Impacts of Climate Change on Agroclimatic Indicators in Iran', *Arid Land Research and Management*, vol. 20, no. 3, 1 September 2006, pp. 245–59.

55 Aye Sapay Phyu and Sann Oo, 'Changing Climate Hurts Myanmar', *Myanmar Times*, 16 December 2009; Mark Kinver, 'Mangrove Loss "Left Burma Exposed"', BBC News, 5 May 2008, http://news.bbc.co.uk/go/pr/fr/-/1/hi/sci/tech/7385315.stm.

56 4AR WG2, p. 92.

57 Vince, 'Coping with Climate Change: Which Societies Will Do Best?'.

58 Soraya Sahaddi Nelson, 'Farming is Latest Casualty in Drought-Stricken Iraq', National Public Radio, 6 August 2008, http://www.npr.org/templates/story/story.php?storyId=93329939;

'Drought New Threat to Stability in Iraq's Diyala', *People's Daily Online*, 21 April 2009; 'Droughts, Dams Force Iraqi Farmers to Abandon Crops', Radio Free Europe/Radio Liberty, 2 October 2009, http://www.rferl.org/content/Drought_Iranian_Dams_Force_Iraqi_Farmers_To_Abandon_Crops/1842000.html.

59 Matthew Savage et al., *Socio-Economic Impacts of Climate Change in Afghanistan*, Report to the Department of International Development, Executive Summary, DFID CNTR 08 8507, http://www.livelihoodsrc.org/uploads/File/2007447_AfghanCC_ExS_09MAR09.pdf; Jerome Starkey, 'Climate Change Delivers a Boost in Battle against Opium Harvest', *The Scotsman*, 23 April 2008, http://news.scotsman.com/world/Climate-change-delivers-a-boost.4009101.jp; David Mansfield, 'Responding to the Challenge of Diversity in Opium Poppy Cultivation in Afghanistan', in D. Buddenberg and W. Byrd (eds), *Afghanistan's Drugs Industry: Structure, Functioning, Dynamics and Implications for Counter Narcotics Policy* (Kabul: UNODC/World Bank, 2006), p. 51, http://siteresources.worldbank.org/SOUTHASIAEXT/Resources/Publications/448813-1164651372704/UNDC_Ch3.pdf.

60 Bates et al., *Climate Change and Water*, pp. 87–8; Sherry Goodman, quoted in Keith Kloor, 'The War against Warming', *Nature Reports Climate Change*, 19 December 2009.

61 Oli Brown and Alex Crawford, *Rising Temperatures, Rising Tensions: Climate Change and the Risk of Violent Conflict in the Middle East* (Winnipeg, MB: International Institute for Sustainable Development, 2009).

62 Rotberg, 'The New Nature of Nation-State Failure', pp. 92–3.

63 Susan E. Rice, 'Global Poverty, Weak States and Insecurity', The Brookings Blum Roundtable, 2 August 2008, available at http://www.brookings.edu/papers/2006/08globaleconomics_rice.aspx, pp. 6–7.

64 Library of Congress, Federal Research Division, *Country Profile: Colombia* (Washington DC: Library of Congress, February 2007), http://lcweb2.loc.gov/frd/cs/profiles/Colombia.pdf; *The CIA World Factbook,* updated 15 January 2010, https://www.cia.gov/library/publications/the-world-factbook/geos/co.html; *IISS Strategic Survey 2009* (Abingdon: Routledge for the IISS, 2009), pp. 113–17.

65 Institute of Hydrology, Meteorology and Environmental Studies (IDEAM), *Colombia – Integrated National Adaptation Plan: High Mountain Ecosystems, Caribbean Islands and Human Health* (Bogotá: IDEAM, 2005), http://www.ideam.gov.co/INAP.pdf.

66 Lobell et al., 'Prioritizing Climate Change Adaptation Needs for Food Security in 2030'; Edward H. Allison et al., 'Vulnerability of National Economics to the Impacts of Climate Change on Fisheries', *Fish and Fisheries,* 4 February 2009, doi: 10.1111/j.1467-2979.2008.00310.x.

67 Jonathan A. Patz et al., 'Impact of Regional Climate Change on Human Health', *Nature,* vol. 438, no. 7,066, 17 November 2005, pp. 310–17; Anastasia Maloney, 'Climate Change is Affecting Colombia's Glaciers and Public Health', Alertnet, 22 September 2009, http://www.alertnet.org/db/an_art/59877/2009/08/22-171019-1.htm; IDEAM, *Colombia – Integrated National Adaptation Plan.*

68 Raymond S. Bradley et al., 'Threats to Water Supplies in the Tropical Andes', *Science,* vol. 312, no. 5,791, 23 June 2006, pp. 1,755–6.

69 *Ibid.*

70 Ricardo Lozano, head of IDEAM, quoted in Anastasia Moloney, 'Climate Change is Affecting Colombia's Glaciers and Public Health'.

71 Ashley Hamer, 'Authorities Begin Water Rationing Ahead of Predicted Drought', *Colombia Reports,* 11 December 2009; Angela González, 'Colombia's Rivers Run Dry', *Colombia Reports,* 25 January 2010, http://colombiareports.com/colombia-news/news/7842-colombias-rivers-run-dry.html; Heather Walsh and Jose Orozco, 'Colombia, Venezuela Cocoa Crops Hurt by Drought, Set to Drop', Bloomberg.com, 14 January 2010, http://www.bloomberg.com/apps/news?pid=20601086&sid=azC9KINdbm4s; Alexander Cuadros, 'Colombia's Inflation Rate May Rise to 11-Month High on Drought', *Business Week,* 5 February 2010.

72 Jeremy Morgan, 'Latin American Realpolitik: Colombia Cuts Electricity to Venezuela, Ecuador', *Latin American Herald Tribune,* 7 February 2010.

73 *Strategic Survey 1998–99* (Oxford: Oxford University Press for the IISS, 1999), pp. 215–20; *Strategic Survey 1999–2000* (Oxford: Oxford University Press for the IISS, 2000), pp. 233–41; *Strategic Survey 2008* (Abingdon: Routledge for the IISS, 2008), pp. 368–70; *Strategic Survey 2009* (Abingdon: Routledge for the IISS, 2009), pp. 345–7.

74 Gunilla Ölund Wingqvist and Emelie Dahlberg, 'Indonesia Environmental and Climate Change Policy Brief', Department of Economics, University of Gothenburg, 8 September 2008, p. 9,

available at http://www.sida.se/Global/ Countries and regions/Asia incl. Middle East/Indonesia/Environmental policy brief Indonesia.pdf.

75 Agus P. Sari et al., *Executive Summary: Indonesia and Climate Change*, Working Paper on Current Status and Policies (Jakarta: PT. Pelangi Energi Abadi Citra Enviro, 2007), pp. 3–4.

76 Wingqvist and Dahlberg, 'Indonesia Environmental and Climate Change Policy Brief', pp. 8–9.

77 Sari et al., *Executive Summary: Indonesia and Climate Change*, p. 5.

78 Wingqvist and Dahlberg, 'Indonesia Environmental and Climate Change Policy Brief', p. 9.

79 Rosamond L. Naylor et al., 'Assessing Risks of Climate Variability and Climate Change for Indonesian Rice Agriculture', *Proceedings of the National Academy of Sciences*, vol. 104, no. 19, 8 May 2007, pp. 7,752–7.

80 *Ibid.*; Alwin Keil et al., 'Water Determines Farmers' Resilience towards ENSO-related Drought? An Empirical Assessment in Central Sulawesi, Indonesia', *Climatic Change*, vol. 86, nos 3–4, February 2008, pp. 291–307.

81 Allison et al., 'Vulnerability of National Economics to the Impacts of Climate Change on Fisheries'.

82 For an assessment of Indonesia's level of food security see World Food Programme, *Executive Brief: Indonesia Food Security*, February 2007; see also http://www.wfp.org/countries/ Indonesia.

83 Arief Anshory Yusuf and Herminia Francisco, *Climate Change Vulnerability Mapping for Southeast Asia* (Singapore: Economy and Environment Program for Southeast Asia, 2009), p. 13.

84 See Angel Rabasa and Peter Chalk, *Indonesia's Transformation and the Stability of Southeast Asia* (Santa Monica, CA: RAND, 2001), http://www. rand.org/pubs/monograph_reports/ MR1344/ for an incisive discussion of the geopolitical importance of Indonesia, written at a time when its trajectory was still very much in doubt. In the event they proved overly pessimistic in their prognosis, although their analysis remains valid.

Chapter Five

1 UNFCCC, Article 2, http://unfccc.int/ resource/docs/convkp/conveng.pdf.

2 TAR, p. 71.

3 Richardson et al., *Synthesis Report*, p. 12.

4 *Ibid.*, p. 16; Joel B. Smith et al., 'Assessing Dangerous Climate Change through an Update of the Intergovernmental Panel on Climate Change (IPCC) "Reasons for Concern"', *Proceedings of the National Academies of Science*, online Early Edition, 26 February 2009, http://www.pnas.org/content/ early/2009/02/25/0812355106.full.pdf.

5 4AR WG1, p. 13 (SPM), adjusted to take into account pre-twenty-first century warming.

6 See Dupont, 'The Strategic Implications of Climate Change'; 'Climate Change: Security Implications and Regional Impacts', *Strategic Survey 2007*; James Lee, *Climate Change and Armed Conflict: Hot and Cold Wars* (Abingdon:

Routledge, 2009); Cleo Paskal, *Global Warring: How Environmental, Economic, and Political Crises Will Redraw the World Map* (London: Palgrave MacMillan, 2010); Gwynne Dyer, *Climate Wars* (Toronto: Random House Canada, 2008); Richardson et al., *Synthesis Report*, pp. 12–17.

7   See, for example, Mazo, 'Thinking the Unthinkable', *Survival*, vol. 50, no. 3, June–July 2008, pp. 249–56; Jim Hansen, 'The Threat to the Planet', *New York Review of Books*, 13 July 2006, pp. 12–16; Mark Lynas, *Six Degrees: Our Future on a Hotter Planet* (London: Fourth Estate, 2007).

8   Richardson et al., *Synthesis Report*, p. 18.

9   'Copenhagen Accord Faces First Test', *IISS Strategic Comments*, vol. 16, comment 1, January 2010.

10 John M. Broder, 'Countries Submit Emission Goals', *New York Times*, 2 February 2010.

11 4AR WG2, p. 364.

12 *Ibid.*, p. 407. For Colombia's per capita GDP see *Military Balance 2010* (Abingdon, Routledge for the IISS, 2010), 94; other estimates put the figure just below $6,000.

13 See Adger et al., 'Successful Adaptation to Climate Change Across Scales'.

14 Lobell et al., 'Prioritizing Climate Change Adaptation Needs for Food Security in 2030'.

15 Dell et al., 'Climate Shocks and Economic Growth: Evidence from the Last Half Century'.

16 Christa Marshall, '"Coal Country" Poses the Biggest Obstacle in Senate Climate Debate', *Climatewire*, 2 November 2009, http://www.eenews.net/public/climatewire/print/2009/11/02/1.

17 For nuanced discussions of the problem of uncertainty for planners see

Michael Fitzsimmons, 'The Problem of Uncertainty in Strategic Planning', *Survival*, vol. 48, no. 4, Winter 2006–07, pp. 131–46; Colin Gray, 'Coping with Uncertainty: Dilemmas of Defense Planning', *Comparative Strategy*, vol. 27, no. 4, July 2008, pp. 324–31.

18 4AR WG1, pp. 854–7.

19 *The Military Balance 2010*, pp. 378, 380.

20 *Ibid.*, p. 380.

21 Evelyn Leopold, 'UK Puts Climate Change in U.N. Council', Reuters, 17 April 2007, http://www.reuters.com/article/idUSN1736824820070418.

22 'National Security Implications of Global Climate Change', Pew Center on Global Climate Change, August 2009; '"Bin Laden" Blames US for Global Warming', BBC, 29 January 2010, http://news.bbc.co.uk/1/hi/world/south_asia/8487030.stm.

23 Oli Brown, *Climate Change and Forced Migration: Observations, Projections and Implications*, Human Development Report Office Occasional Paper (Geneva: UNHDR, 2007), http://hdr.undp.org/en/reports/global/hdr2007-2008/papers/brown_oli.pdf.

24 United Nations High Commissioner for Refugees, *2008 Global Trends: Refugees, Asylum-seekers, Returnees, Internally Displaced and Stateless Persons* (Geneva: UNHCR, 2009), p. 2.

25 US Department of Defense, *Quadrennial Defense Review Report*, February 2010, p. 84, available at http://www.defense.gov/QDR.

26 Balgis Osman-Elasha, 'Building Resilence to Drought and Climate Change in Sudan', in *State of the World 2009: Into a Warming World* (Washington DC: Worldwatch Institute, 2009), pp. 92–5.

27 For a discussion of the problems of and a framework for development

in fragile states, see Zoellick, 'Fragile States: Securing Development'. See also Manish Bapna et al., *Enabling Adaptation: Priorities for Supporting the Rural Poor in a Changing Climate*, WRI Issue Brief (Washington DC: World Resources Institute, May 2009).

28 Martin Parry et al., *Assessing the Costs of Adaptation to Climate Change: A Review of the UNFCCC and Other Recent Estimates* (London: International Institute for Environment and Development and Grantham Institute for Climate Change, 2009), pp. 9, 14. Parry et al. gave the figures as £4-37bn and £86-109bn.

29 *Ibid.*, p. 8. The lower figure is from the Stern Report and the higher from the UN Development Programme.

30 Rob Young, 'UN Kyoto Climate Change Fund Still to Help Poor Nations', BBC News, 9 December 2009, http://news.bbc.co.uk/1/hi/business/84033377.stm.

31 See http://climatefundsupdate.org.

32 See http://unfccc.int/files/meetings/cop_15/application/pdf/cop15_cph_auv.pdf.

33 Nathanial Gronewold, 'Red Tape, High Fees Hamstring Int'l Green Funds', *New York Times*, 22 December 2009. For a detailed critique of the finance provisions of the Copenhagen Accord, see J. Timmons Roberts et al., *Copenhagen's Climate Finance Promise: Six Key Questions*, IIED Briefing (London: International Institute for Economic Development, February 2010), http://www.iied.org/pubs/pdfs/17071IIED.pdf.

34 Zoellick, 'Fragile States: Securing Development', p. 82.

35 Rice and Patrick, *Index of State Weakness in the Developing World*.

Conclusion

1 Ron Suskind, *The One Percent Doctrine* (New York: Simon & Schuster, 2006), p. 62.

⌒IISS ADELPHI BOOKS

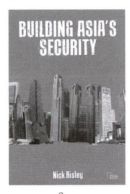

ADELPHI 408

Building Asia's Security

Nick Bisley

ISBN 978-0-415-58266-7

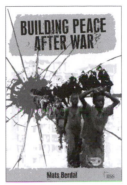

ADELPHI 407

Building Peace After War

Mats Berdal

ISBN 978-0-415-47436-8

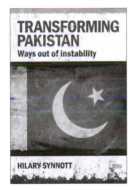

ADELPHI 406

Transforming Pakistan:
Ways out of instability

Hilary Synnott

ISBN 978-0-41556-260-7

ADELPHI 404–5

China's African Challenges

Sarah Raine

ISBN 978-0-415-55693-4

All Adelphi books are £9.99 / $19.99

For credit card orders call **+44 (0) 1264 343 071**
or e-mail **book.orders@tandf.co.uk**
Orders can also be placed at **www.iiss.org**

Routledge
Taylor & Francis Group

Adelphi books are published eight times a year by Routledge Journals, an imprint of Taylor & Francis, 4 Park Square, Milton Park, Abingdon, Oxfordshire OX14 4RN, UK.

A subscription to the institution print edition, ISSN 0567-932X, includes free access for any number of concurrent users across a local area network to the online edition, ISSN 1478-5145.

2010 Annual Adelphi Subscription Rates		
Institution	£457	$803 USD
Individual	£230	$391 USD
Online only	£433	$763 USD

Dollar rates apply to subscribers in all countries except the UK and the Republic of Ireland where the pound sterling price applies. All subscriptions are payable in advance and all rates include postage. Journals are sent by air to the USA, Canada, Mexico, India, Japan and Australasia. Subscriptions are entered on an annual basis, i.e. January to December. Payment may be made by sterling cheque, dollar cheque, international money order, National Giro, or credit card (Amex, Visa, Mastercard).

For more information, visit our website: **http://www.informaworld.com/adelphipapers.**

For a complete and up-to-date guide to Taylor & Francis journals and books publishing programmes, and details of advertising in our journals, visit our website: **http://www.informaworld.com.**

Ordering information:
USA/Canada: Taylor & Francis Inc., Journals Department, 325 Chestnut Street, 8th Floor, Philadelphia, PA 19106, USA. **UK/Europe/Rest of World:** Routledge Journals, T&F Customer Services, T&F Informa UK Ltd., Sheepen Place, Colchester, Essex, CO3 3LP, UK.

Advertising enquiries to:
USA/Canada: The Advertising Manager, Taylor & Francis Inc., 325 Chestnut Street, 8th Floor, Philadelphia, PA 19106, USA. Tel: +1 (800) 354 1420. Fax: +1 (215) 625 2940.

UK/Europe/Rest of World: The Advertising Manager, Routledge Journals, Taylor & Francis, 4 Park Square, Milton Park, Abingdon, Oxfordshire OX14 4RN, UK. Tel: +44 (0) 20 7017 6000. Fax: +44 (0) 20 7017 6336.

The print edition of this journal is printed on ANSI conforming acid-free paper by Bell & Bain, Glasgow, UK.

0567-932X(2009)49:6;1-V